SILVER HIGHWAY

A Celebration of the Trans-Canada Highway

WES RATAUSHK

Fitzhenry & Whiteside
195 Allstate Parkway
Markham, Ontario L3R 4T8

The author and publisher would like to acknowledge the assistance of
Minolta Canada Inc.
Ford of Canada
in the development of this project.

Book design: Darrell McCalla
Additional Photographs
John Devaney
D. Lorente
Typesetting: Jay Tee Graphics Ltd.
Printed and bound in Hong Kong

Canadian Cataloguing in Publication Data

Rataushk, Wes
  Silver highway

Produced in conjunction with the Silver Highway
Photography Contest, sponsored by Minolta Cameras.
ISBN 0-88902-729-3

1. Trans-Canada Highway — Description and travel —
Views. 2. Canada — Description and travel —
1981-   — Views. I. Title.

FC75.R3 1987   971.064'7'0222   C87-094681-1
F1017.R3 1987

Silver Highway, Golden Dreams

by Norm Rosen, Editor, Photo Life Magazine

When our ancestors met in Charlottetown more than 120 years ago to forge
a new Canadian dream, one of the cornerstones of confederation was the
concept of a single railway line, linking all Canadians from coast to coast. As
the nation expanded westward, the dream was forged into reality, and
Canadian unity came to be symbolized by the frontier spirit of long journeys
through distant provinces.

As the automobile replaced the railway as the main mode of personal travel,
the goal of a single highway linking Canadians from coast to coast was born.
Twenty-five years ago, this dream of a single road from Atlantic to Pacific, a
Trans-Canada Highway, was inaugurated.

Over the years, the Trans-Canada Highway has been the road to freedom
and adventure for millions of Canadians. Traversing the nation's most
populous regions, it is the private citizen's favourite route for business travel,
pleasure trips, and interprovincial migration. In times of economic upheaval,
the Trans-Canada Highway has been the route from regional unemployment
to boom town euphoria. In times of prosperity and national celebration, it has
been the road to the discovery of Canada's national identity — from Expo '67
in Montreal in our centennial year, to the recent Expo '86 in Vancouver,
Canadians don't hesitate to travel from coast to coast to participate in special
events. The Trans-Canada Highway has been the key to this penchant for
family mobility for the past generation, and it will continue to link Canadians
for many generations to come.

This year, Canada celebrates the silver anniversary of the Trans-Canada
Highway. How fitting it is that the road has been transformed from a mere
line on a map of the nation, to the artery through which the soul of the
nation pulses. Along the highway, proud Canadians have erected monuments
to the beauty of their regions, commemorating sites and celebrating events in
Canadian history. The Big Nickel in Sudbury, the Canada goose in Wawa,
the world's largest fish in Kenora, the moose in Dryden, the Vegreville
Pysanka, and many more examples of civic pride, are all designed to be
viewed from the Trans-Canada Highway.

Our highway has also been the route of Canadian heroes. Terry Fox, whose
tragic battle with cancer ended his Marathon of Hope in Thunder Bay, is
remembered in a monument at a most spectacular location along the shore of
Lake Superior. His feat inspired other Canadians: Steve Fonyo, who realized
the dream of a cross-country run, and Rick Hansen, whose Man In Motion
tour covered not only the entire Trans-Canada Highway, but the well-
travelled roads of many other nations of the modern world as well. These
heroic feats have only been a few of the recent events confirming that courage
and dedication are qualities inherent in the Canadian identity.

The Trans-Canada is a route to adventure. For Canadian families setting out
on a toll-free tour of the dominion, or harried commuters travelling through
winter white-outs to reach their homes, each kilometre offers a new
experience along a highway that is certainly the most impressive in the world.

Continued overleaf . . .

Commemorating the twenty-fifth anniversary of the Trans-Canada was a dream for Wes Rataushk, but the story of the highway must also reflect the great spirit of the Canadian people. To provide an overall perspective on the effect the Trans-Canada Highway has on the lives of Canadians, a photo contest was organized, with a selection of the visual images to be included in this book. As Editor of Photo Life Magazine, it was my privilege to have been associated with this aspect of the Silver Highway project along with Minolta Canada, the official sponsor of the contest. It is indicative of the love of travel inherent in the Canadian spirit, that the photographs presented here as contest winners include an image of Grand Falls, New Brunswick, photographed by Joseph Brooke of Langley, B.C. and a Banff vista by Leo McDonald of Annapolis, Nova Scotia. Surely this demonstrates the role this wonderful highway plays in our national love of intercontinental travel.

The Trans-Canada Highway links Canadians, but as we celebrate the 25th anniversary of its completion, it is obvious that the highway transcends its original raison d'être. It has become much more than just a road — for those who are familiar with its many personalities, it is a vibrant, beautiful creation dedicated to the freedom to travel without restriction from coast to coast. It is a shining example of the spirit of Canadian life — totally free from horizon to horizon; a concrete symbol of the Canadian lifestyle.

Silver Highway
Photography Contest Winners

First Prize Maxxum 7000 with 50 mm f/1.7 lens and gadget bag
(3 prizes awarded)

Dr. Van E. Christou	**Herb Noren**	**Joseph C. Brook**
Lethbridge, Alberta	Salmon Arm, B.C.	Langley, B.C.

Second Prize: Minolta Freedom III compact autofocus camera
(10 prizes awarded)

Donald Zemaitis	**Barb McDougall**	**Edna M. Larrabee**
Lindale, Alberta	Victoria, B.C.	North Vancouver, B.C.
Bruce Symington	**Stan Kruk**	**Bill Crosby**
Thunder Bay, Ontario	Calgary, Alberta	Richmond, B.C.
Dave Reede	**Ben Oueck**	**François Audy**
Winnipeg, Manitoba	Calgary, Alberta	St. Gedeon, P.Q.

Leo MacDonald
Annapolis Royal, N.S.

Silver Highway
Photo Contest Winner
Tree in ice storm, **Dr. Van E. Christou**

Following page
Silver Highway
Photo Contest Winner
Grand Falls, New Brunswick, **Joseph C. Brook**

2nd Following page
Silver Highway
Photo Contest Winner
Shuswap Lake from Sicamous, British Columbia, **Herb Noren**

THE NEW YORK TIMES — *August 5, 1962*
The opening last week of the final link in the chain of roads comprising the 4,860-mile Trans-Canada Highway signaled the beginning of a new era for motorists traveling across this sprawling country. With the completion of the rugged ninety-two-mile Rogers Pass Highway, it is possible at last to drive with relative ease from St. John's, Nfld., all the way to Victoria, B.C.

The opening of the route, built at immense cost and effort, is an historic occasion for Canada. The event will be formally observed on Sept. 3, when Prime Minister John Diefenbaker will unveil a special memorial at Rogers Pass, in the Canadian Rockies, commemorating the linking of Canada's Atlantic and Pacific shores.

CANADIAN PRESS — *September 3, 1962*
Prime Minister John Diefenbaker declared the Trans-Canada Highway officially open to traffic at 3:05 p.m. today.

The ceremonies at the summit of Rogers Pass . . . came 12 years after the first construction was begun on the 4,860 mile cross-country highway.

Not too many years before America began its quest to put a man on the moon, it was impossible for Canadians to cross the country on reliable roads. While the superpowers raced to the stars, Canada achieved a more down-to-earth but equally daunting goal — the completion of an all-paved, nearly eight thousand kilometre highway stretching from coast to coast and across all ten provinces.

A federal-provincial agreement — called "An Act to Encourage and Assist the Construction of a Trans-Canada Highway" — authorized construction of Canada's national highway, starting December 10, 1949. Cost estimates put the federal price tag at $150 million, and, as far as the experts were concerned, the job was to be completed in seven years. Time wore on and costs escalated to such a level that a 1956 amendment to the Trans-Canada Highway Act provided that Canada pay half of all construction costs, plus ninety percent of the price of the most difficult ten percent of each provincial route. By the time the Trans-Canada was officially opened in 1962, the overall cost had crept close to a billion dollars. When the last mile was paved and constructed to Trans-Canada Highway Act specifications, in May, 1971, the price (to Canada and the provinces) had climbed to 1.4 billion. The money bought Canada the longest paved highway in the world — a road that was passable every day of the year.

The highway links Victoria to St. John's. Via Nanaimo, Vancouver, New Westminster, Kamloops, Revelstoke, Banff, Calgary, Medicine Hat, Swift Current, Moose Jaw, Regina, Brandon, Portage la Prairie, Winnipeg, Kenora, Thunder Bay, Orillia, Peter-borough, Ottawa, Montreal, Lévis (and Quebec City), Rivière-du-Loup, Fredericton, Moncton, Charlotte-town, Truro, North Sydney, Corner Brook and Gander. Starting in St. John's, where Devon fishermen founded Canada's oldest city, the Trans-Canada spans Newfoundland, boldly going where no road ever went before. Ships ferry vehicles to Nova Scotia and the highway crosses to Bras d'Or Lake, summer home of Alexander Graham Bell. Near Pictou, another ferry crossing leads to Prince Edward Island and Charlotte-town, where the precepts of Confederation were hammered out. In New Brunswick, the highway leads past Moncton to the heart of Fredericton, one of the nation's most beautiful capitals. Northward, the road joins the old Témiscouata Trail to Quebec, and follows along the south shore of the St. Lawrence. From Montreal, pavement runs next to historic fur trade routes to Ottawa and North Bay, past the nickel mines of Sudbury and on to the Soo. After the locks at Sault Ste. Marie, the Trans-Canada enters newly-conquered territory: Wawa and Marathon to Thunder Bay and through Kenora to the fields of Manitoba. Winnipeg draws highway traffic to the centre of town, and then sends it westward across the prairies — Regina, Swift Current, Medicine Hat. After hundreds of kilometres of straight smooth driving, Calgary's Trans-Canada approaches the shadow of the Rockies. The road climbs past peaks, glaciers and canyons to Rogers Pass and sweeps down to the dry valleys of Kamloops and Cache Creek, curving alongside the Fraser River, and running smoothly beyond Hope to Vancouver. One more ferryboat shuttles traffic across the Strait of Georgia. Then it's through Nanaimo and over the Malahat Pass, and 7,891 kilometres are completed in Victoria. As the road started in a very British city on an island in the Atlantic, so it ends in a very British city on an island in the Pacific.

The Trans-Canada Highway project was jointly undertaken by the federal and provincial governments, and called for combining existing roads (sometimes improving them) with newly constructed routes, where necessary. Insofar as it was possible, the highway was to provide the most direct route across Canada, on a line within 320 kilometres of the U.S. border. After all, prior to the 1960s, most cross-Canada motor transport was via the safer U.S. super highways nearby. If the Trans-Canada was to compete for the trucking business, it would have to be easily accessible and not far from the existing U.S. transport routes.

Canadians had lobbied for an all-weather, all-Canadian highway route for generations. In the nineteenth century, when Canada wooed British Columbia to join the fledgling Dominion, the western colonists hinted that they would join Canada if a railway joined the west coast to the Great Lakes. B.C.'s governor offered a compromise, saying that he'd sign the Dominion agreement if Canada built a wagon road connecting Vancouver with Winnipeg. In fact, Ottawa went for the big deal, and cut a transcontinental railway through the Rockies. A road became unnecessary.

In 1910, pioneer western motorists formed the Canadian Highway Association to promote a cross-country road. Two years later, A.E. Todd, a resident of Victoria, offered a gold medal to the first person who could drive from coast to coast. That same year, Englishman Thomas Wilby sought adventure (and the medal), and attempted the first Trans-Canada "highway" drive. Starting from Halifax on August 27th, Wilby set off for the west. After fifty-two tortuous, vehicle-wrecking days, the adventurer limped into Victoria and ceremoniously emptied a flask of Atlantic seawater into the Pacific. Although Wilby made a tidy profit from a popular book he published about the journey, Todd's gold medal was not his. Many of Wilby's northern Ontario miles were travelled inside a Canadian Pacific Railway freight car, and other segments were completed by driving on railway tracks or floating on lake steamers.

By the 1920s, many Canadians were car owners, and Dr. Perry Dolittle, president of the Canadian

Automobile Association, was travelling to every province of the country, appealing for national highway support. While the auto association lobbied provincial and federal governments, private industry staged the major campaign that was to be the impetus for a transcontinental highway. On Ford of Canada's twenty-first anniversary, the auto company employed photographer Ed Flickenger to cross Canada by car.

On the morning of September 8, 1925, Flickenger dipped the rear wheels of a shiny new Model-T into the Atlantic, near Halifax, Nova Scotia. Flickenger vowed, by hook or by crook, to get across Canada in that car. It was a "Vancouver or Bust" expedition and, over most of the trip, the country did everything it could to bust the photographer's car.

The Model T travelled a few hundred kilometres, at most, on paved roads. The rest of the trip was over dirt tracks, some so narrow that trees and bushes gouged the car's sides. In northern Ontario, Flickenger clocked up to thirty kilometres on a good day's driving, over rocks and enormous potholes. Like a Red River cart settler, he searched riversides for shallow fords. The vast prairies turned out to be an endless run through axle-deep gumbo, and precipitous tracks through the Rockies were often life-threatening.

British Columbia's mountains and northern Ontario's Lakehead foiled the explorer's hopes of travelling across Canada by rubber tire. About 1,300 kilometres of country were devoid of roads or pathways — except for the transcontinental railway tracks. With the Canadian Pacific Railway's help, Flickenger outfitted his Model T with flanged wheels and hoisted it on the tracks, to cross these otherwise impassable miles.

On October 17th — forty days after leaving Halifax — Flickenger inched his front wheels into the Pacific waters at Vancouver, British Columbia. And, even if he *had* relied on the kindness of C.P.R. strangers, Flickenger had made history. He crossed the 7,670 kilometres — from coast to coast — without once leaving Canadian soil.

Twenty one years later, Brigadier R.A. MacFarlane drove a new Chevrolet for nine days over 7,700 kilometres from Louisbourg, Nova Scotia to Victoria, B.C. The trip from coast to coast, on rubber tires (at the cost of only four flat tires), was finally accomplished and Todd's medal was won. But even MacFarlane's trip was more a stunt than a practical exercise. It was time for a serious talk about building a reliable, decent highway right across the country.

The Trans-Canada Highway Act became law in 1949. Thirteen years later, Prime Minister John Diefenbaker proudly declared the Trans-Canada Highway open to all traffic. Over the next twenty-five years, a good number of Canadians packed the family car and drove from coast to coast. Today highway travellers still drive the TCH and marvel at the colour of Canada — the green pastures of British Columbia, blue prairie skies, the ice-cold silver gleam of a northern Ontario winter morning. The highway shows the country exactly as the country is — it brings us face to face with every season and every landscape that is Canada.

Although the days of "goin' down the road" from coast to coast died with the sixties, virtually all of us have driven at least some part of the Trans-Canada, watching the landscape change from muskeg to mountain to endless prairies, experiencing through bloodshot and tired eyes, the diversity of Canada. For Canada *is* different when seen from the road. It's longer, grander, and deadlier. It's comforting, dangerous and hospitable. It pleases all of the people some of the time and maybe even some of the people all of the time. We get out of it what we put into it, as the kilometres tick by.

The Trans-Canada follows historical paths. It rides over the famous east-west trails of Canada's explorers and pioneers. It passes maritime settlements of the Acadians and Loyalists, and it flows arm-in-arm with Quebec's and northern Ontario's voyageur lakes and streams. In the west, the highway connects what were Hudson's Bay Company and R.N.W.M.P. forts — now travelling past modern Hudson's Bay Company stores and R.C.M.P. depots — and it nudges up to time-honoured railway tracks through the Rockies and

Selkirks, before joining with British Columbia's famed Caribou Wagon Trail to the sea.

The going may be smooth now but, in the 1950s, engineers and highway workers experienced just how miserable this land could be. To overcome formidable difficulties, an army of power shovels, bulldozers, graders and dump trucks was assembled. The men who operated this equipment sometimes found that even an earth-mover made little headway. In parts of northern Ontario and Newfoundland, muskeg was fifty feet deep, entailing the pouring of thousands of tonnes of rock fill to form a solid base. Even the flat prairies proved difficult in the rainy season, when sticky, heavy gumbo gooed everything to a halt. Five thousand tonnes of explosives had to be used to blast two million tonnes of rock, all to complete one fourteen kilometre stretch of roadbed between Field and Golden, British Columbia. And no one knows how many million litres of mosquito and black fly repellent were slapped on the arms of road crew workers.

In Newfoundland, Canada came closest to thwarting ambitious highway engineers. Muskeg deep enough to swallow an earth-mover had to be filled with thousands of tonnes of rock, to provide a solid pavement base. Much of the 864 kilometre route was cut through virgin territory where no road of any kind had existed. Over rock outcrops and through peat bogs, road crews were forced to blast and fill — sometimes to ten metre depths — virtully the entire length of the route.

In Quebec, a tunnel under the St. Lawrence, at the Trans-Canada entranceway to Montréal became complex — pouring concrete segments on dry land and then sinking each piece into place. In all, less that one mile of highway cost seventy-five million dollars to build — and then sink!

Nine-tenths of Canada's people live near the slender belt of the Trans-Canada Highway. But before this national road existed, major segments of the path were written off as inaccessible. Two formidable gaps had to be spanned along Ontario's northern route. The first was quite simply bridged in 1959, when a short route was cleared and paved near Parry Sound. The big job — demanding four years of back-breaking, equipment-crushing labour — was northward between the Agawa River and Marathon, Ontario. A 264 kilometre gap existed along a wild, rugged terrain of rock outcroppings, dense forest and gorges. To begin, men and equipment were flown in or barged up on Lake Superior. While struggling with the roadbed, huge pieces of equipment vanished in the muskeg. At the time, an engineer was quoted as saying, "One evening we finished a two mile stretch of paving over a muskeg and by morning the entire road had sunk out of sight!" In the end, twenty-five bridges were built to span the fast-running rivers and dark ravines. Finally, these 264

kilometres of rugged Precambrian shield were accessible to more than just foot traffic. The gap in Canada was no more.

Just west of Winnipeg, near the Assiniboine River, sticky quagmire and constant valley flooding threatened immediate construction and future highway rights of way. The solution was to build a bridge on dry land, and then channel the previously uncooperative river along a less flood-prone route and under the new bridge.

Aside from problems with sticky gumbo during spring rains (twenty-five years earlier it took fourteen hours to drive through sixty-four kilometres of axle-deep quagmire) Saskatchewan's and Alberta's routes proved "easy" to build. The major obstacles lay ahead in western Alberta. But while Albertan crews looked with trepidation at the Rockies, Saskatchewan's road workers celebrated the completion of the Trans-Canada Highway's provincial segment in 1957. D.A. Lamour, chief engineer of the Saskatchewan Department of Highways, remembered, "We got the last five mile stretch paved at noon on October 31. By two o'clock it had blown up a blizzard, the ground froze solid and we couldn't have got in another lick of work until the following April!" Just in the nick of time, on October 31, 1957, the Trans-Canada Highway was one down, nine provinces to go.

In British Columbia, the 147 kilometre Rogers Pass route cut 160 kilometres off the tortuous Big Bend Highway through the Selkirk Mountains. Before 1962, motorists endured the Big Bend — then called the "world's longest detour" — in order to drive from Revelstoke to Golden, B.C. Drivers travelling to Golden from Revelstoke were forced to head due north for 72 kilometres, make a complete U-turn, and drive due south, travelling a total of 307 kilometres to a point about eighty kilometres east of where they started. On top of horrendous back-tracking, the Big Bend was open only a few short months each summer and was often barely passable during the open season. Those who drove the Big Bend told stories of passing rusting wrecks of other cars, dodging rock slides, fording mountain run-offs, crawling along cliff edges, bouncing over washboard and teeth-rattling potholes, and inching up steep grades.

To circumvent Big Bend, engineers plotted a route through Rogers Pass, following existing Canadian Pacific Railway track. Where the rails hid from avalanches in the eight kilometre Connaught Tunnel, the highway route was exposed. The C.P.R. had long abandoned the 1,400-metre high track bed after, over a thirty-year period, 236 railway workers perished beneath crushing avalanches. Cynics say the railway eventually chose the tunnel route because of the high cost of replacing track and snowsheds each winter season, not because of the high cost of lives.

The Trans-Canada was to attempt these mountain paths. The route, even though it was laid on top of abandoned railway grades, proved to be the most expensive segment along the national highway and in fact became the most expensive road ever built.

In its time, the Rogers Pass project was widely hailed as an engineering feat of the first magnitude. But, like the Seven Wonders, the feat was accomplished by anonymous engineers, by the scarred hands of unknown workers. Along a single fourteen kilometre segment of the pass route, two million tonnes of rock and another couple of million tonnes of earth were removed by these hands.

Much of the cash for this most expensive segment of the Trans-Canada was spent on engineering and devices for snow and avalanche control. This is avalanche country, as deadly and dangerous as can be found anywhere on earth. And the pass traditionally records Canada's heaviest snowfalls. Lacking funds to pay for long kilometres of tunnels, the Trans-Canada engineers devised an interlocking system of snow sheds, diversion mounds and an avalanche control operation, in order to keep Rogers Pass open year-round.

The official opening of the Trans-Canada Highway — conducted on September 3, 1962 by Prime Minister John Diefenbaker before an audience of three thousand — took place not in Ottawa, but at Rogers Pass. The side was chosen for its "defile of boundless beauty," its miracle of engineering and because it was a few kilometres away from another historic site — Craigelachie, B.C. where, in 1885, Sir Donald Smith drove the C.P.R. transcontinental's last spike.

A brochure prepared for the official opening praised the ingenious engineers who plotted this route through the dangerous Selkirk Mountains. In the government's words, "The route through Glacier National Park, from the viewpoint of the engineer as well as the tourist, is the showplace of the entire Trans-Canada Highway . Here, the highway clings to the mountainsides as it cuts through the towering Selkirks and provides motorists with some of the most magnificent scenery to be found anywhere in the world. And when you combine towering mountains with heavy snowfall, the result is dangerous avalanches. However, this danger has been well taken care of by the ingenuity of the highway builders who have designed and constructed in the area a unique system of avalanche defences. The result is a standard of safety at least as high as that for the best

mountain highways in the world."

The brochure waxed eloquent about Canada's great achievement, but the official opening event became strangely comical. Princess Patricia's Canadian Light Infantry Band was on hand to play "O Canada," but they were an orchestra without music — their instruments truck got lost on the road between Calgary and Rogers Pass. Politicians federal and provincial attempted to out-do each other in the field of rhetoric, and their speeches ran nearly an hour over schedule. "Flying Phil" Gaglardi, British Columbia's fire and brimstone Minister of Highways, thanked God *personally* for the beautiful weather that day. The minister from Saskatchewan, perhaps confused by soaring mountains, expressed pleasure at being in Quebec.

In the end, Prime Minister Diefenbaker said a few "all's well that end's well" words, and cut the ribbon. After decades of public hopes, and more than ten years of construction, it was possible for Canadians to travel right across the country in the comfort of their own cars.

Those of us who travel this giant road embark on an epic journey across six time zones, through prairie, wilderness and mountain, and at the widest parts of the North American continent. Anyone who has driven long stretches along the highway is familiar with the common emotions: the thrill of a natural wonder; the anger of being caught behind an endless stream of camper trailers; the evening relief of stumbling out of the car after 1200 hard-driving kilometres. Some say you don't embark on a Trans-Canada trip, you enlist. Drivers are constantly in danger of smashing into a wayward moose, skidding on a bridge that iced before the rest of the roadway, being hit by falling rocks. Travelling across the second largest country on earth isn't easy, but the rewards are great.

The Trans-Canada, along most of its path, is not a divided superhighway like America's freeways. But it doesn't try to be. The Trans-Canada is, rather, Canada's Main Street and, in an unassuming way, pulls itself around more than a fifth of the circumference of the planet, at this latitude. The great highway of Canada is twice as long as the Great Wall of China. Beyond the urban congestions of motels, fast food restaurants and self-serve gas bars, the Trans-Canada leads its wanderers along cliffs that take the breath away, through landscapes that sigh with gentle beauty and beneath the crushing power of mountainsides laden with unstable snow.

BRITISH COLUMBIA

Mile "0" sign, Beacon Hill Park, Victoria, British Columbia

The highway begins and ends at "Mile 0" in Victoria's Beacon Hill Park, where bonfires once directed ships away from an offshore ledge and into Victoria's snug harbour. A signboard dedicated by the Canadian Automobile Association marks its terminus. Near the "Mile 0" sign, Beacon Hill Park's heights drop over a steep cliff face to the Pacific Ocean but, typically Victorian, the cliffs have been civilized with stairs and polite warnings to "watch your step," on the descent to the sea. America lies across Juan de Fuca Straits — faint, foreign and blue the Olympic rainforest of Washington State.

Standing with my back to the United States, I looked beyond the "Mile 0" marker to . . . what? Canada? I had grown up in this country, but still had not seen much of it. I had not set foot in Prince Edward Island or Quebec City. Mainlanders joked about Newfoundland. I had never been to Newfoundland, but I had joked about it too. I had seen the world, but practically nothing of Canada. I felt the desire to travel across the country on one grand tour. It made me excited because I knew so little — but was to learn much. I started the car and drove off to look for Canada.

Douglas Street, the major thoroughfare through downtown Victoria, is named for the first governor of the colony, Sir James Douglas. He was also the man who chose Victoria as the Hudson's Bay Company's Pacific coast headquarters in 1842. On Douglas, near centre town, is an imposing set of British Columbian symbols — stately native longhouses and carved totem poles. Aptly named Thunderbird Park (the Thunder-

bird is a common totem figure), the small green contains well-preserved examples of west coast poles, many carved by famed native artist and chief Mungo Martin.

I discovered that Thunderbird Park borders on one of Canada's best museums. The facade of the British Columbia Provincial Museum reveals no clue to the fantastic exhibits inside. Constructed in the 1960s (not a high period of architecture), the provincial museum portrays British Columbia's social and natural history. The way in which history is displayed makes the museum a priceless gem.

In 1972, the Provincial Museum opened its first major exhibit, a modern history exhibit that used a "you are there" technique to transport visitors into another time and place. Dusty display cabinets gave way to living exhibits that people could touch and enter. Today, the 1.2 million annual visitors to the complex don't walk past exhibits, they walk into an old west town, a west coast canning factory and a Haida Indian village.

In another gallery, an enormous wooly mammoth stands guard on the glacier-covered terrain of ice-age British Columbia. Through a corridor of ice, a path leads to a quiet rainforest where deer and other forest animals stand almost within reach. Beyond the forest, the trail leads to the oceanside, where seals and sea lions bask in the sun. Beyond are the murky ocean depths. Other exhibit areas meticulously re-create, with remarkable accuracy, the sailing vessels that brought the first European explorers to this coast, old-time mining camps, a native settlement and a town from British Columbia's wild west past.

'Empress Hotel, Inner Harbour, Victoria, British Columbia

While the sights, sounds and smells of these galleries transport you into another time and place, across the street British Columbia's political leaders debate modern problems inside a historic building that recalls another, more Victorian time.

British Columbia's Parliament Buildings were designed by wet-behind-the-ears twenty-five-year-old Francis Rattenbury, who thereafter designed the Empress Hotel and the Crystal Garden — in fact, the core of stately buildings surrounding Victoria's inner harbour. Rattenbury beat out sixty-one competitors in a contest for the building's design, held in 1892. It's said that the young architect bamboozled judges, by claiming he had designed a great many buildings in Britain. Actually, this structure was his first major commission.

The 1893 parliament buildings are best seen at night, when they are illuminated by thousands of tiny, sparkling lights. Perched above, on the highest cupola, shines the golden figure of George Vancouver, the English man who explored these parts in 1778.

Victoria seems proud to be known as Canada's last bastion of the British Empire. In the downtown "tourist" core, where shiploads of American visitors disembark for a day in the Commonwealth, the few maple leaf flags are outnumbered by hundreds of Union Jacks. Tour buses are overhauled London double-deckers, and the favourite Victoria souvenir is a tin of Scottish shortbread.

Victoria is a major tourist magnet because of the Canadian Pacific Railway's early marketing efforts. As the railway was wont to do, it built a hotel worthy of its honoured passengers and named it the Empress. Since 1905, tea in the Empress' grand entrance hall has

been an essential part of gracious living — and gracious travelling. The Trans-Canada runs behind the dowager Empress. The imposing turreted bulk of the Empress encourages highway travellers to park and visit, even though they may have been on the road for less that a kilometre since leaving Beacon Hill Park.

Victorian London was famous for its Crystal Palace. In British Columbia, Victorians fondly remember learning to swim at Crystal Garden. Once the largest salt water indoor pool in the Commonwealth, and constructed as an amenity for guests of the Empress Hotel across the street, the pool is now a tropical garden. Where children paddled, scarlet macaws squawk to flamingos roosting under palm fronds.

The first hundred kilometres of Trans-Canada Highway, between Beacon Hill Park and Nanaimo, winds through rain forests rising from volcanic rock, past gulf island harbours and shrouded inlets. From the roadside to the horizon you can see ten shades of green. In many ways, Vancouver Island looks like the little bit of England it pretends to be. The fields exactly duplicate the countryside of southern Britain.

Shortly after leaving Victoria, the road climbs a mountain pass known as Malahat Drive. The highway here is often shrouded in a road-hugging mist typical of west coast rain forests. A thick coat of moss upholsters rock cliff faces that tumble down to the roadway's edge. Beyond the asphalt, the cliffs drop hundreds of metres into the sea. Across the inlet, stands of four hundred year old Douglas fir and western red cedar coat the Saanich Peninsula. To the west, high peaks shine in their crisp white coats of glacial ice and snow. A dozen kilometres past the Malahat summit, the path drops quickly to the rolling acres of the south-central island.

Vancouver Island has long relied on tourism to boost its economy, drawing visitors from across Canada and the Pacific Northwest. Butchart Gardens may be the most famous visitor attraction, but hopeful entrepreneurs have set up weird and wonderful establishments to compete for the tourist dollar. North of the Malahat, the Trans-Canada passes by the Glass Castle, a complex made entirely of empty beer and wine bottles. Nearby is Blackie's Autoparts, with a sign encouraging visitors to stop and view more that 10,000 hub caps. The creative spirit lives!

Duncan, at the halfway point between Victoria and Nanaimo, lies in the Cowichan Valley. In the early years of white settlement, Scottish immigrants taught the Cowichans how to knit Shetland-style wool sweaters. In turn, the Indians incorporated traditional symbols and totems into the sweater patterns, and today Cowichan knit sweaters are highly prized for their warmth and beauty of design.

Duncan is the major trading centre on this part of the island. Its surrounding valley is an agricultural anomaly in Canada, with a long growing season that makes two or three crops a year possible.

Northward, near the highway community of Ladysmith (set smack on the forty-ninth parallel), signs point to a short feeder road leading to Chemainus, billed as the "little town that could." Once a dying forestry town, swamped in unemployment, the town spent its last dollars employing island artists to paint huge murals on major buildings. Today, people from around the world stop to view these murals, and tourism supports the town.

Near Nanaimo, the Trans-Canada runs beside tiny Petroglyph Park, a provincial reserve protecting ancient Indian carvings on a soft, sandstone rock face. As at similar sites across the country, sections of the carvings have been defaced by those who want everyone to know that they were here. A thousand years from now, will these grafitti be as archaeologically important as the Indian pictographs are today?

Soon, the highway passes through Nanimo and near a historic harbour and Hudson's Bay Company Bastion. Built in 1853, to protect British Columbia's first coal mine, the Bastion now overlooks a city which no longer has coal, but survives on shipping and forestry.

Travelling north through town, I could see that Nanaimo has a graspable size, a sense of civic pride, even a modest grandeur. The road passes numerous chowder houses and a marine industrial area, on the way to Departure Bay some two kilometres north. Departure Bay is the stepping off point from Canada's far-western island. Here the Trans-Canada leads directly onto a B.C. ferry, to cross the Strait of Georgia.

Just beyond Departure Bay, the ships pass tiny Snake Lake, to the south. Here cormorants, black oystercatchers, pigeon guillemots and glaucus-winged gulls nest on the rocky outcropping, the sea protecting the eggs and fledglings from predators. As we passed near the island, a cormorant flew slowly above the cliffs and gulls nagged behind our vessel.

The *Queen of Alberni*, one of the largest ships in the world's largest ferry fleet, makes eight daily crossings between Horseshoe Bay in West Vancouver and Nanaimo's Departure Bay. On the morning that I made the crossing, I watched the captain pilot his boat out into the Strait of Georgia, as a disembodied voice from "Vancouver Coast Guard radio" blared over the wheelhouse speakers.

The seas were calm during this run, but I learned that, on a crossing earlier that day, fifty-five knot winds had battered the hull. The spray from a fifty-five knot wind can shatter a vehicle's windshield. On other occasions, dense fog blankets the coast, making the job of piloting a 140 metre, three hundred-vehicle ferry a tense occupation.

A B.C. ferry captain soon learns that the greatest hazard on the Strait of Georgia runs, is the challenge of pleasure boating. It's been said that Vancouver's citizens own the most boats per capita in Canada. On a breezy summer day, the sun sparkles on the yachts, tipping toward Vancouver. It's a lovely sight, but a ferry captain sees the small boats as an obstacle course through which his ship must thread.

Beyond the pleasure-sailing waters, pods of killer whales, sea lions and harbour seals come as a more welcome diversion to the wheelhouse officers. Ignoring (or, perhaps, showing off to) the ferries, killer whales rise out of the blue-green waters, their paths forming graceful arcs through the air, as they turn nose to tail and plunge beneath the surface.

Travelling at twenty knots to keep fuel consumption down to a miserly $7,000 a day, her engines thumping at 9,800 horsepower, the *Queen of Alberni* travels between Departure Bay and Vancouver in a little over an hour and twenty minutes. In a year, she will repeat this journey more that 1,400 times, and carry a significant number of B.C. Ferries's annual eight million passengers.

At Horseshoe Bay, the ferries unload and, within minutes, reload for a return voyage. Horseshoe Bay, a tiny fishing village, is actually part of the Municipal District of West Vancouver, which, in turn is part of Greater Vancouver (known to the people of these parts as the "Lower Mainland"). Vancouverites give their areas and monuments names familiar only to them; a municipal jargon unheard of elsewhere. They call Lion's Gate Bridge the "First Narrows" and the Trans-Canada Highway the "Upper Levels," a description of the route's climbing path alongside steep mountainsides. No matter what the names, the Upper Levels TCH is tailor-made for showing off Canada's most spectacularly situated city.

Between West Vancouver's Horseshoe Bay and Burnaby's East Hastings Street, the Trans-Canada crosses through some of Canada's most beautiful country — climbing with the Upper Levels along the gritty cliffs of Seymour, Grouse and Hollyburn mountains, and past memorable bays and fishing coves. Along the Upper Levels route, thousands of metres of rock cuts were needed to lay the Trans-Canada Highway. It's not just the mountains, cliffs and sea breezes, it's all the engineering — the iron imbedded in rock — that makes it marvellous.

At the eastern edge of West Vancouver, strands of fist-thick cable can be seen on Lion's Gate Bridge, which connects the beaches of Ambleside to the dense city forest of Stanley Park. Across Lion's Gate and through Stanley Park is central Vancouver — Canada's third largest city and home to half the population of British Columbia. Back in 1886, Vancouver was surrounded by thick forests. Notwithstanding that, the one-month-old town asked the federal government to give it a 405 hectacre wooded peninsula in Burrard Inlet, for use as a public park. The government agreed, and today Stanley Park is a rare urban woodland surrounded by highrises and the sea.

Beyond Stanley Park, downtown Vancouver's shining office towers and the crowded apartment buildings of it west end fight for the best views of the sea. English Bay curves around it all, softening the harsh angles of the skyscrapers. Early morning joggers circle the seawall, a path winding along the shoreline, as ocean freighters wait in English Bay for the call to load or unload their cargoes.

Across the bay are the Spanish Banks, named for the Spanish Captain José Maria Navaez, who entered these waters a full year before George Vancouver arrived in 1792. Perched above the steep banks are concrete towers of learning — the University of British Columbia's schools of agriculture, forestry and oceanograpy and its famous Museum of Anthropology.

North of the Upper Levels Highway are sheer rock walls and deeply cut canyons. The Trans-Canada crosses Capilano Canyon. Within batting distance is Capilano Suspension Bridge, an attraction billed as the world's greatest suspension footbridge. Patros cross a 137 metre wood and wire rope structure hanging seventy metres above the Capilano River's raging waters. On the canyon's far side, huge Douglas firs, red cedar and hemlock surround quiet walking paths in a west coast rainforest. Back across the swinging bridge is a collection of totem poles dating from — well, the park owners don't exactly know. They did tell me that some of the poles were ancient when they were

RCMP Constable Vic Vanderveer, Upper Levels Highway, North Vancouver, British Columbia

brought to the park in the last century.

Capilano Road funnels traffic from the Upper Levels Highway to a parking lot at the base of Grouse Mountain. From there an aerial tram car takes visitors and skiers 1,100 metres up the mountain for a spectacular panoramic view of greater Vancouver.

The Trans-Canada bisects the city of North Vancouver, cutting south down a long, winding hill and finally crossing Indian Arm, the most southerly fiord on the B.C. coast, via the Second Narrows Bridge. Below the Second Narrows, ship-builders toil and giant grain elevators rise. On one side of the elevators, rail tracks lead to the prairies. On the other, a deep water port for ships travelling to the Far East.

Torontonians say they are the worst drivers in Canada. Calgarians, Montrealers and Vancouverites tell similar tales about their highway drivers. To find out about Vancouver's Trans-Canada traffic, I rode with Constable Vic Vanderveer of the R.C.M.P. highway patrol. ·

On the force for seventeen years — seventeen months of that on highway patrol — Vanderveer is one of twenty-one officers patrolling a stretch of highway that should require a force twice that size. At least, it seems like that when you're on this job. As Vanderveer says, "Some days you'd think that people don't have any common sense at all. I've stopped people who said they were speeding because it was too foggy to see the speed

limit signs."

When stopping a "client," Vanderveer routinely calls in the speeder's license plate number, so a dispatcher can check the license with computer data for outstanding warrants or theft. There is another purpose for reporting the license. "If something happens to me, whether I be shot or hit or beat up, they have a license number to go on," Vanderveer said. Even a simple task like stopping a speeder can be a life and death encounter. "I've got enough scars to prove that this job isn't always that much fun. I've saved lives and it feels good. I've taken a life . . . it doesn't feel so good."

Heading east one fall morning, under a typical Vancouver sky — dull, grey and moody, with a mist hanging low enough to rest on the road surface — travelling from here to St. John's, Newfoundland seemed an impossible task. But, as with all grand encounters, each day was to be so filled with concentrated driving, curious people and fascinating places that the long-distance goal became less daunting — a day-to-day unveiling. The Trans-Canada Highway is more than a long, unchanging superfreeway. It's a connection of local roads — each segment reflecting a regional lifestyle.

Spanning the Fraser River, traffic crosses a graceful and enormous arch called the Port Mann Bridge. Longest of 781 structures built for the Trans-Canada Highway, the Port Mann stretches more that two kilometres. Here, at the eastern edge of Vancouver, the Fraser River is wide and tame. Not far away, the Trans-Canada hugs another side of this same river, where canyon walls squeeze river water into deadly, frothing rapids.

Beyond Abbotsford, Vancouver's influence fades away, and the highway shoots straight through a wide farming valley on the way to Chilliwack. Here, the sight of people falling from the sky is common. Chilliwack airport, although not nearly as famous as Abbotsford Field (home of the continent's biggest annual air show), is popular with skydivers. Small planes circle above the Fraser Valley at 2,400 metres, and deposit tiny black specks into the sky. Forming star, chain and circle patterns, the specks drop, grow in size and eventually become people, hanging beneath colourful parachute canopies. The bright parachute cloth stands out vividly agains the green foothills of the Coast mountain range.

The Trans-Canada cuts through a gap in this grassy wall, as it passes public gardens and visitor attactions, such as Bridal Veil Falls, a high, wide curtain of water falling some twenty-five metres from a sheer cliff. Soon the trail leads to the town of Hope ("beyond Hope" is the local joke). Hope was the terminus for pack trains bringing furs from Fort Kamloops. From here, fur bales were taken downriver to Fort Langley and the ships bound for Europe.

The Fraser River was named for Simon Fraser who, in 1808, was the first European to pass this way. Old Simon, smart enough to abandon impossible overland travel, canoed this river to the sea.

Upriver, and wedged in a high valley between the Coast Mountains and the Cascades, is Yale, a town with a rollicking past. Once this was a city of 20,000. Today it is tumbledown but still beautiful, and home to a couple of hundred citizens. Formerly a roaring gold rush town, Yale today is a misty village of fading memories. On a hillside below the Trans-Canada, is Yale's Pioneer Cemetery, a moody collection of blackened headstones surrounded by a thick stand of trees, which dampen traffic noises. The graves rest in a meadow that, a century and a half after its clearing, is being reclaimed by the forest. The bodies of those pioneers who cleared the forest at Yale are now part of the returning woodland.

Yale is also the beginning of British Columbia's 1862 Caribou Wagon road, which transported thousands of hopefuls to the northern gold fields in Barkerville. For nearly a hundred kilometres, the modern Trans-Canada follows, and sometimes runs over, this pioneer trail. At a cost of 1.5 million dollars in the 1860s, the Caribou Road put the colony of British Columbia deeply into debt; a situation which, in no small part, persuaded B.C. to join Canada.

Beyond Yale, the Fraser River and its environs change complexion. For nearly a hundred kilometres, the Trans-Canada Highway snakes along a terrible and beautiful path, lined on one side by glistening rock cliff faces and the other by the fierce Fraser River waters. The canyon walls, separating Coast and Cascade Mountains, rise higher as the river runs faster and more turbulently.

Near the growling Fraser is the town of Spuzzum, sporting one of the most intriguing names along the national route. Spuzzum has a café, a gas station and a sign that reads, "Thanks for Visiting Spuzzum — Come Again." What more could you ask?

At the oldest house in Spuzzum, no more than a log shack, John Allen MacKinnon talked to me about old times. MacKinnon is a native Canadian whose father took on his father's Scottish name. As a wood fire crackled in an iron stove, he sat in a living room just barely wider that his height. Between solitaire hands, he spoke of colder, harder times when he shovelled tons of snow from blocked-in locomotives. Life was hard here in the early 1900s. MacKinnon showed the stooped shoulders and blinded eye which were the consequences of railroad and woodsman work that paid a dollar a day and a bowl of soup.

The struggle between canyon walls and Fraser River waters reaches its climax at Hell's Gate, a narrow gorge that forces a river wanting to be a thousand metres wide into a thirty metre corridor. Hell's Gate squeezes the Fraser River into such contortions that water blasts away at the very rock confining it. Back when the Trans-Canada Highway was an infant, entrepreneurs strung an airtram over the boiling waters of Hell's Gate and today thousands of tourists cross the gorge to enjoy restaurants and shopping on the other side.

North of Hell's Gate and the town of Boston Bar, the highway passes through numerous rock slide areas. Saplings barely grab a mountainside toehold before more scree cuts a swath through their bed. The rock slide terrain continues through to a town called Lytton named after the author and British Colonial Secretary Edward Bulwer-Lytton, who penned the immortal line, "It was a dark and stormy night . . . " Lytton's claim to fame is temperature. The highest maximum temperature in British Columbia pushed Lytton's thermometers to 44°C (111°F). Here, the Trans-Canada breaks eastward out of the Fraser Canyon, and traces the route of another of British Columbia's notorious waterways, the Thompson River.

At Ashcroft, a historic building sits at the Trans-Canada's edge. The lodge was built in 1863, as a roadhouse, by the Cornwall brothers. They also started a cattle ranch, believing that supplying miners might be more profitable than digging for gold. They were right. Behind the Cornwalls' white wood manor are squalid sod shacks, "home" for the Chinese labourers who served roadhouse guests. Today, the shacks are part of a free museum that recalls times and conditions

of the mid-nineteenth century in British Columbia.

It's a short hop from Ashcroft, along Kamloops Lake, to the city of Kamloops, an industrial centre for British Columbia's interior. The Trans-Canada skirts the southern edge of Kamloop's sagebrush-covered, desert valley, and travels onward through small tourist-oriented waterfront communities, hugging Shuswap Lake. Along the line is the community of Sicamous (pronounced sick-a-moose), a contender in the great Trans-Canada goofy name contest.

The Trans-Canada runs within a few dozen metres of one of the country's most famous sites — Craigellachie, the spot where the east and west links of the transcontinental railway were joined. The last spike was pounded into place here on November 7, 1885 by Donald Smith, Director of the C.P.R. Accounts say that, after Smith drove the final iron nail home, there was a moment of silence, and then a great cheer rose among the men. The stubborn Canadian and Chinese labourers who pushed these five thousand kilometres of steel rail across a continent did the job in four years, beating the TCH team by nearly a decade.

Revelstoke sits at the edge of the Selkirks, some of the most rugged mountains in British Columbia. Throughout Mount Revelstoke National Park, freakish peaks tower above hanging valleys, massive glaciers and canyons. In the town of Revelstoke, homes are protected by steeply-sloped roofs designed to allow the heavy snow to slide off before it exerts too much pressure on outer walls.

East of Revelstoke, a stone marker was erected "To commemorate the official opening of the Rogers Pass route of the Trans-Canada Highway between Revelstoke and Golden, completed July 30, 1962 by the Province of British Columbia and the Government of Canada. An achievement by men of ingenuity, skill and determination. Rogers Pass in the Selkirk Mountains was discovered by Major A.B. Rogers, Canadian Pacific Railway Mountain Division Chief Engineer, on May 25, 1881 with a party of Indians from Kamloops. The following year he crossed through the pass on foot. Let all who use this highway look with awe and reverence upon the majesty the God-given beauty of these mountains. Hon. W.A.C. Bennett, Premier Hon. P.S. Gaglardi, Minister of Highways." The cairn marks the site of a ceremony staged by the B.C. government, which was calculated to take the steam out of federal dedication ceremonies at Rogers Pass summit, barely a month later. Even today, British Columbians and some history books claim the Trans-Canada Highway officially opened on July 30, not September 3, 1962.

The climb through Rogers Pass in Glacier National Park evokes strong emotions. For someone like me, who grew up in the shadow of high mountains, the journey

Yoho National Park, British Columbia

is a wonderful experience, almost sensual. For others, those who love the wide expanses of the prairies, the mountain climb can be uncomfortable; they feel closed in by dangerous peaks. How could one stand amid all this towering beauty and not feel diminished. One man did — a Saskatchewan farmer who was heard to say, "The mountains are alright, I guess, but they sure do block the view!"

The Selkirks not only block the view, they bring death and destruction rumbling down their steep declines. Throughout Rogers Pass, avalanche paths — corridors in the dark forest — can be seen on either side of the Trans-Canada. In spring, travellers will spot bears on these slopes, searching for animals killed months earlier by a falling wall of snow, ice and debris.

The big deal is snowfall. In Rogers Pass, an average winter sees ten metres of snow pile on the mountains. In a bad year, you'll get fifteen metres or more. This means that any time during the winter, an avalanche can rumble down and close off the highway.

Canadian Pacific Railway engineers constructed wooden snow sheds in the 1880s to protect trains passing through the Rogers Pass avalanche zone. But they didn't work. After years of destroyed wooden sheds — culminating in a 1910 avalanche that killed sixty-two people — the railway was forced to give up and burrow underground through the Connaught Tunnel in Mount Macdonald. C.P.R. left the pass to its madness.

Forty years later, Canada again looked at keeping a year-round transportation route open through Rogers Pass, and engineers were hired to develop new methods of protecting the public.

They primary highway defence against slides turned out to be "dragon's teeth," a system of earth mounds that was first developed during WWII to block the movement of tanks and armoured vehicles. Now they would block the advance of snow and ice. Where dragon's teeth were unnecessary, a bench defence series of trenches was used in conjunction with diverting dams, to channel slides away from the roadway. The most evident defence works seen by today's drivers are the concrete and steel snow sheds that cover dangerous slide areas. While winter traffic hums through the sheds, tons of snow may be rolling over these structures and tumbling into the abyss below. But snow shed construction was expensive (this part of the Trans-Canada was the project's most expensive segment; one kilometre, over a million 1962 dollars) and offered too little protection.

At Rogers Pass Summit is a double-arched monument commemorating the official dedication of the Trans-Canada Highway on September 3, 1962. It seemed appropriate to dedicate the road at its most costly point. Near the monument is a collection of A-frame structures, built to withstand heavy snowfalls outside and inside, to house Canada's snow fighters.

The senior officer of the Rogers Pass Avalanche Control Operation is Fred Schleiss. He has worked in these mountains since 1959. In those days, when the Trans-Canada was still only a concept, Schleiss and his brother were hired by the federal government to develop an effective avalanche control system. A background in avalanche survey, gained in his native Austria, made Schleiss virtually the only person in Canada capable of developing this program to keep the national highway open year-round. In 1959, little was known about avalanche control, and Swiss experts told Canada it was crazy to think of running a year-round highway through these mountains. Fred Schleiss set out to prove them wrong.

During the days of rail lines along this route, there were nearly eleven kilometres of wooden snowsheds. In the 1960s, cost were too great to consider more that about two kilometres (approximately five percent of the avalanche-prone section) of concrete snowsheds. They had to find another way to combat the deadly snowslides.

The first idea was simple enough. Early in the season, operatives pre-planted dynamite charges on avalanche-prone slopes. The dynamite would be triggered when snow accumulations were heavy, but before they threatened to close the highway. However, grizzly bears in the area quickly developed an appetite for explosive charges, which reduced the effectiveness of pre-planting them. Strangely, the bears seemed to suffer no ill effects from their dynamite diet. The next solution was to shoot down the offending snow packs.

A howitzer was purchased — a World War II 105 mm howitzer, modified to shoot down unstable snow packs. Converted to fire with pinpoint accuracy, the Rogers Pass Avalanche Control operation's three howitzer cannons are fired by a contingent of Canadian Forces troops, under the command of Schleiss and his operatives. In summer, when most Canadians travel through this pass, circular concrete platforms can be seen on either side of the bare highway. These are gun placements, where the howitzers are anchored and swung round, to aim at the targets of snow.

When unstable layers of snow pack are detected, the big guns are wheeled from their lairs and fired at a trig-ger zone, which brings the layer of unstable snow crashing down a mountainside. Schleiss — who asks no one else to play this particular game of Russian roulette — sits in the slide path and watches, more often listens, to see if the trigger was effective. "In most cases we shoot in heavy snowstorms with nil visibility, so listening to a slide is more important that seeing. After a few years of practise, you can hear that the avalanche was triggered properly; the slide's rumble tells you if the hazard has been taken out." The snow-covered section of highway is plowed and roadblocks are lifted, to allow impatient drivers their right of way.

Schleiss says that the system works, "partly because of decades of knowledge mixed with a strong dose of luck, and so there have been no highway traveller avalanche fatalities through these mountains," Still, the danger of a killer avalanche exists every year and in fact an avalanche on January 8, 1966 killed two control officers. Parks Canada employees sometimes walk a fine line between life and death to keep the Trans-Canada running free.

Beyond Rogers Pass, at the banks of the Kicking Horse River, is the community of Golden. Heading east from Golden are views of the sharp-pointed, fantastic mountains (thirty of them are higher than three thousand metres) of Yoho National Park.

Yoho Park is not as well-known as Banff. Even so, it contains some of Canada's most dramatic and spectacular Rocky Mountain wonders. Not the least of these are Emerald Lake, the Spiral Tunnels (tunnels in Cathedral Mountain constructed to make railway grades less critical, by increasing overall distance travelled) and Takakkaw Falls. Yoho is a Cree expression of astonishment and Takakkaw means "it is magnificent." Takakkaw Falls are the highest falls in Canada, dropping uninterrupted for 381 metres before smashing into the Yoho River.

Yoho National Park's boundary is also the British Columbia-Alberta border. At the point where the Trans-Canada crosses into Alberta, it enters Canada's most famous park and continues on through a storybook landscape.

ALBERTA

The Alberta boundary marks the start of Canada's most famous nature preserve, Banff National Park. Bear, elk, mountain goat, bighorn sheep, moose, wapiti, wolf — and nine million visitors a year.

Mile-high Lake Louise, the first site of note along Alberta's Trans-Canada, is probably the best-known spot in the country. Looming over the lake, Mount Victoria and Victoria Glacier dominate the view. In the foreground, the waters of Lake Louise seem to shimmer in the quiet mountain air. Most people are moved to silence at the sight. The words of Tom Wilson, the first white man ever to view the panorama, said it best — "As God is my judge, I never in all my explorations . . . saw such a matchless scene."

Not as well known as Lake Louise, Moraine Lake is situated a few kilometres away. The lake was named by an early Banff-area mountain man, Walter Wilcox, who gave the lake its name because he suspected the pools was caused by a moraine that dammed a glacial runoff. To this day, geologists argue whether the dam is a true moraine or the result of a rockslide off the Tower of Babble, a peak rising over Moraine Lake's northeastern shore. No matter what the geological cause, Moraine Lake is one of those places where every traveller feels like a discoverer who is seeing it for the first time. There are few such places on earth.

From Lake Louise to Banff townsite, the Trans-Canada hugs the side of Castle Mountain (which, for about thirty years, was renamed Mount Eisenhower as a Canadian tribute to America's wartime hero). "Castle" is an appropriate name for the fortress-like formations of this peak's immense cliffs. In the same line of sight, Mount Temple rises to 3,543 metres, which is a record of sorts; this is the highest mountain in the Bow Range.

The road through Banff Park is a combination of bends and high-speed straights, streams on one side, crags on the other. It curves past Mount Corey in the Sawback range, where you can see, about three hundred metres down from Corey's peak, at Hole in the Wall, an enormous natural cave forming a gaping hole in Corey's side. Years ago, Freemasons held secret meetings within its cool darkness.

Banff is what most of the world imagines when it thinks of Canada. The oldest and largest of townsites in the country's mountain parks owes its existence to the discovery of mineral hot springs on the slopes of Sulphur Mountain. Cave and Basin Hot Springs, a short drive from the Banff townsite, is also where the national park system in Canada began. To thwart C.P.R. surveyors' attempts to turn the site into a private, money-making attraction, the Canadian government declared the Cave and Basin Hot Springs, and about four hectares of land surrounding it, the country's first nature preserve. Seven decades later, a major reason for choosing the western route for the new TCH was to provide easy access to Canada's first (and greatly expanded) national parklands.

Hot pools at Sulphur Mountain are the favourite swimming holes in Banff Park. Even the Upper Hot Springs' malodorous fumes fail to deter the ten of thousands of bathers who annually swim there under the shadow of swinging cable cars that carry tourists to Sulphur Mountain's peak. Signs suggest that twenty minutes is the maximum time one should swim in the water — too much of this good thing is not recommended.

An outdoor gallery surrounds the hotpool. This is where the less adventurous park visitors (during cold months, clad in winter parkas and mitts) watch their companions sweat in the vaporous waters below. The afternoon I was there, gallery watchers were so intent on ogling the swimmers that no one was aware of a mule deer not a half-dozen metres away placidly munching on mountain grass.

Down the mountainside, at the edge of Banff townsite, is a natural history museum that has remained virtually unchanged since 1925. This is the oldest museum in the west, with collections dating to 1895. Its building was constructed at the turn of the twentieth century. As carefully preserved as the park, the Banff Natural History Museum and its contents reveal changing attitudes in ecological preservation. When these collections were assembled, animals were executed for display, especially those species, such as the wolf or lynx, that were predators of game animals.

Banff was named for Banffshire in Scotland, the birthplace of one-time C.P.R. President George Stephen. A hundred years later, the C.P.R. still exerts a major influence over the townsite, because of its castle in the Rockies—the Banff Springs Hotel. The first Banff Springs Hotel was constructed in 1888 and after various expansions and reconstructions the Scottish-baronial-French-château structure remains nestled in Banff's mountain slopes. Hosting celebrities and guests, who faithfully return year after year, the Banff Springs Hotel is one Canadian landmark that does justice to its worldwide image. And the world takes note; Banff is the second busiest tourist town (after Niagara Falls) in the country.

North of the Trans-Canada and just east of Banff townsite is Bankhead, a town full of memories. A coal miners' community, it was prosperous in the early decades of the twentieth century but, because of declining markets and labour-management strife, lost its one and only industry, when the mines were shut down. Shortly thereafter, the townsite was ordered removed by park officials. What remains are the skeletons of brick-and-stone processing buildings and rusting coal cars. The townsite is gradually being reclaimed by

nature. Just out of sight, vehicles speed along the final stretches of the Trans-Canada's path through eastern Banff National Park.

On the eastern slopes of the Rockies, the highway passes by Exshaw, a one-industry village surviving on the fortunes of cement processing. Almost immediately beyond Exshaw, the great Rocky Mountains drop abruptly to the level of foothills. Here, a big sky opens over far-reaching prairies. There is a rapid alteration in light — a brightness and a clarity that comes from a higher sky not pinched in by mountain peaks. The sunny skies stretch all the way to Calgary.

Running across the spine of Alberta's foothills, Kananaskis Trail bisects the Trans-Canada between Banff and Calgary. Drivers turning off the Trans-Canada southward on the Kananaskis experience the bone-rattling consequences of driving through ranch country. In this region, Texas gates are crossed within a few metres of leaving the Trans-Canada. The gates' iron beams keep cattle and horses at bay, while allowing bumpy passage to vehicles.

Less than a ten-kilometre drive south on the Kananaskis Trail is a singular reminder of the remoteness of this country. Among the modern buildings of a forestry research centre, are a few World War II vintage structures — a guard's tower and "The Colonel's Cabin." Both saw service when this was the site of a prisoner of war camp. Here German soldiers captured in the early months of the war lived under

not too-intensive scrutiny in the foothills of the Rockies. The theory was that if a POW escaped he would never make it out of the rugged area.

Back on the TCH, I approached Alberta's largest city. After the villages of Spuzzum and Bankhead, Calgary looked huge. Scattered over several valleys that drain into the Bow River, the city at twilight glittered like an oasis in a black desert.

Calgary, the city that wishes it was the capital of western Canada—or at least Alberta — is the product of a boom-and-bust economy. More that anything else, Calgary won its spurs with the world's greatest outdoor amusement, the raucous Calgary Exhibition and Stampede. Although outsiders think Calgarians dress-up western only for the annual two weeks' fete, many Calgarians look like cowboys year-round. The Stampede is merely an excuse to yahoo a little louder and more frequently. The real west lives in Calgary and no one looks twice at the sight of a man strutting down the street in cowboy clothes, no matter what day of the year. Businessmen bow to the requirement of suits in the office, but many insist their suits be cut in the traditional western style.

Calgary so embraces the western spirit that its major thoroughfares are called trails rather than freeways. Its covered hockey arena is named the "Saddledome." Driving along 16th Avenue (the Trans-Canada's name in north Calgary, I encountered the epitome of the modern cowboy and steed — a bluejeaned, stetson-

Banff Avenue & Cascade Mountain, Banff, Alberta

wearing guy riding in a pickup truck, complete with gun rack in the rear window. The appliances may be modern, but the soul is part of the old west.

Opposing this wild west image is a 16th Avenue shop called "W.A. Gough, Violin Maker & Restorer." I stepped inside this shop one afternoon, and was transported into the past. Al Gough made his first violin at the age of six. The master violin maker faithfully carries on traditions established by the Amati and Stradivari families hundreds of years ago. Handcarving sprucewood and curly maple, the traditional woods used by generations of Italian violin makers, Gough shapes his own violins and retores ancient instruments. Inscribed on some of the antiques Gough restores is the maxim "In life I was silent, in death now I sing."

As I left the shop, Gough returned to his companions, shaping a plank of curly maple and, as he described it, "carving away everything that doesn't look like a violin." Outside, a heavy tractor-trailer rumbling along 16th Avenue wrenched me back to the present. Following the truck eastward along Calgary's Trans-Canada would take me to Alberta's short-grass prairie, a land where nature is conquered with sweat, determination and millions of litres of water.

Immediately east of Calgary the land flattens out like tea in a saucer. You feel that if you looked hard enough you could probably see Medicine Hat, nearly three hundred kilometres away. The label "Sunny Alberta" is more than appropriate for this part of the country. The sun bleaches even the blue of the sky and, although I drove through the country a few days after heavy rainstorms, the land had quickly sucked in the moisture, leaving a cracked and dry landscape pleading for another drink.

Brooks lies squarely within the great Canadian plains. The town is the centre of Alberta's irrigation lands and a community of tree-lined streets; an oasis in treeless, barren desert-like country. Here water works wonders, as it has since the beginning of the twentieth century when water from the Rockies was diverted through a series of dams, spillways and aqueducts. The water irrigates rich agricultural lands that were once the death of early range animals.

Brooks has a famous pheasant hatchery and wildlife centre, where pheasants are bred and raised for release every fall. Understandably, this makes the area a popular destination for hunters each autumn. Nearby, horticulturists operate an experimental farm, searching for flora that are tough enough to withstand late springs, scorching summers and early frosts.

Very little grows between Brooks and Medicine Hat except cactus, sagebrush and short-grass. There are stretches of the highway where nothing breaks the monotony but a shimmering ribbon of pavement, or the sight and smell of a dead skunk in the road. You can travel for an hour in a straight line; a curve in the highway becomes a major event.

The barren lands north and east of Suffield, Alberta, forty kilometres west of Medicine Hat, were chosen during World War II as a military testing range and training site now called Canadian Forces Base Suffield. At 2,690 square kilometres, CFB Suffield is two thirds the size of Prince Edward Island and NATO's largest military training site in the Commonwealth. At times, more that 16,000 Canadian and British troops practise on this site, conducting rocketry testing, land mine detection and live firing maneuvers.

Set in some of the most inhospitable country along the Trans-Canada, Suffield experiences such temperature extremes as 51°C in August and -47°C in January. But the men and women who work here seem proud of their godforsaken posting. The base commander boasts that "no other NATO range offers the freedom of joint ground and air maneuver with live firing." Conducting a brief tour of the base, Lieutenant Michel Bussière proudly wears the Suffield military crest — a royal crown resting on a wreath of maple leaves surrounding a spitting rattlesnake. Bussière chose the base's motto to describe positive life and training at Suffield — "Out of the Ordinary." Given the harsh climatic conditions and barren, rattle-snake infested lands, out of the ordinary is about the nicest thing most civilians would say about CFB Suffield.

The salt-white road leads from Suffield to the major trading centre of southeast Alberta — Medicine Hat. Medicine Hat is not the funniest community name along the Trans-Canada Highway. Most people prefer Goobies, Newfoundland; South Gut, Nova Scotia; Bagot and East Braintree, Manitoba; Moose Jaw, Saskatchewan or Spuzzum, British Columbia. Nevertheless, the name Medicine Hat caught the ear of a Hollywood scriptwriter in the 1940s and for years afterward any mention of Canada in a Hollywood comedy was accompanied with a snickering reference to Medicine Hat.

The many legends of how this valley was named have been homogenized into one story — the tale of a great battle between the Cree and Blackfoot Indians. The Cree fought bravely until their medicine man turned chicken and high-tailed it across the South Saskatchewan River, losing his headdress in midstream. Believing this to be a bad omen, the Cree put down their weapons and were killed by the Blackfoot. The bizarre victory was commemorated by naming the site "Saamis," which translates as "medicine man's hat."

Medicine Hat's citizens are still in some ways pioneers. Driving along the Trans-Canada, you might spy unusual livestock — Peruvian llamas. True to the pioneer spirit, some ranchers here shun horses, and cattle, and choose to be father, mother and nursemaid to these exotic creatures. Placidly chewing cud and gazing through great, dreamy eyes over the parched landscape, the llamas have take easily to prairie life.

No doubt, were he still alive, Medicine Hat's favourite author would have had something witty to say about llamas grazing on the short-grass prairie. During a 1907 visit, Rudyard Kipling described the town as possessing "all hell for a basement." The community sits atop twenty billion cubic metres of natural gas reserves. In Kipling's time, one could tap a natural gas source merely by drilling at any spot in any part of town. To this day, citizens delight in using Kipling's curse to describe their hometown, and in teasing newcomers with tall tales about the author's favourite North American settlement.

Sharing underground space with natural gas reserves, a preglacial river supplies Medicine Hat's water. Even so, city officials impose alternate days rationing. One can't be too careful with something as precious as water.

The area surrounding Medicine Hat burns under a desert sun. In the late 1850s, Captain John Palliser led a thirsty survey crew through what is now southeastern Alberta. On a July day, he wrote of the pleasantries they encountered . . . "Soil worthless. Found a human skull on the dusted plain. Camped where we killed several rattlesnakes."

In the intervening years, necessity inspired irrigation and today where Palliser saw worthless land are flat green fields where farmers grow sugar beets, potatoes and alfalfa. Medicine Hat supports a huge indoor agricultural industry, which grows vegetables year-round, in greenhouses heated by the city's abundant natural gas reserves. This kind of market gardening is only profitable in a town with all hell for a basement.

Medicine Hat isn't a bad place to be from, and it's certainly a nice place to visit. For those who haven't had the pleasure, the city sends its own special calling card across the continent. The arid climate creates a birthplace and rejuvenation area for numerous cyclones that move across North America.

At the eastern edge of Medicine Hat, the highway nears a point where railway tracks cut near the South Saskatchewan River and slide down a long hill into the city proper. This is the spot where the only Canadian sightings of a phantom train have occurred. In June 1908, C.P.R. crews running locomotives up this hill reported, on two separate occasions, being blinded by an oncoming engine's headlight. An oncoming train was impossible — this was a single-track section and watchmen reported no other engines on the rails. One month later, the engineman who had witnessed both apparitions was killed when his train, descending the hill, collided head on with an engine mistakenly allowed to ascent the tracks.

Driving along the Trans-Canada east of Medicine Hat the short-grass country is tinged with a gentle odour of prairie sagebrush, juniper and prickly pear

Combining in southeastern Alberta

cactus. On hot days, a cowboy will suck on the fruit of the cactus to quench his thirst. Even in the blistering heat of summer wild flowers are everywhere, small and hugging the dust-swept highway embankment. Wild roses (Alberta's provincial flower), milk vetch, lupine, scarlet mallow and the beautiful gaillardia, with their purple-brown bull's-eyes, add splashes of colour to the earth. Above the beauty of this ranching country horned larks sing on the breezes, and a turkey vulture circles high above, riding the currents, waiting for a passing driver to drop dead. No luck this time.

Herds of cattle appear as specks on the fields. This is open rangeland where ranchers, requiring twenty hectares per head of cattle, must share the sparse grasslands. In this country you don't ask of a man, "How big is his ranch?" You ask, "How many calves does he brand?" That"s what matters.

This is one of the few spots along the Trans-Canada where drivers will spot antelope. The prong-horns huddle close to the ground and at first glance appear to be boulders on the prairie. These creatures have telescopic eyesight and if you stop your vehicle at the roadside they'll move out at speeds up to eighty kilometres per hour. Obviously, pronghorn antelope are among the most difficult Trans-Canada creatures to photograph.

Roughly twenty-five kilometres further along, just south of the highway, the antelope sometimes gather near a marker honouring the first member of the North West Mounted Police to be murdered. On November 17, 1879, Constable Marmaduke Graburn was discovered near this spot with two neat bullet holes in the back of his head. The accused, a Blood Indian named Star Child, was found not guilty by a jury of settlers who feared reprisals from the unfriendly Bloods. Constable Graburn was avenged a few months later, when Star Child died of tuberculosis.

With the ghosts of Star Child and Constable Graburn on my tail, I crossed the boundary between Alberta and Saskatchewan. The journey continued on to Canada's breadbasket.

SASKATCHEWAN

Captain John Palliser made a monumental mistake regarding western Canada. In 1857, Palliser, in the employ of the Hudson's Bay Company, led a survey party across the vast flatlands of the prairie provinces. He reported that the landscape was "desert or semi-desert . . . which can never be expected to become occupied by settlers."

Palliser was proven wrong many times over. Although Saskatchewan is still sparsely populated, the land offers bountiful harvests. So bountiful that neither markets nor storage can be found to absorb its annual yield.

On the Trans-Canada Highway in Saskatchewan, the other cars seemed to be moving much faster than elsewhere. Of course it was only natural that a driver should hurry through land as flat as a floor. It was too easy to speed through this countryside; I made strict rules in order to slow myself down.

When I did ease off the accelerator, I saw beautiful things. Just after dawn, the sun played on the landscape in unusual patterns and hues. Unlike the golden tinge of a sunrise, the early morning light at times shot the highway through with a silver glow that shimmered in the distance.

Motoring in Saskatchewan's early morning mist brought to mind thoughts of the dirty thirties, with their grit-blasting dust storms and devastating loss of topsoil. I spoke to one farmer who remembered the time when generations of history blew away with the wind. As a young boy, he would collect arrowheads and flint knives, finding hundreds of them over the years. When the topsoil blew away, he explained, "they were left lying right on the hardpan." Aside from parched derelicts of abandoned farm houses, few remnants of those years remain. A handful of windmills, erected during the dustbowl years when power for electricity and pumping water was supplied by the incessant wind, can still be seen from the Trans-Canada roadside.

Just beyond the Alberta-Saskatchewan border, the road climbs over a slight rise. There at the crest, lies the vast, flat expanse of the Saskatchewan prairie. This territory is monumental in its emptiness. In summer the sun is so bright that it arcs above the horizon and sears the landscape; in winter the stars cast a cold light over a frozen countryside.

Under the washed-out sky, signs in southeastern Alberta and southwestern Saskatchewan direct traffic to the Cypress Hills and the famous North-West Mounted Police detachment, Fort Walsh. Rising to nearly 1,400 metres above sea level, the lodgepole pine-covered Cypress Hills mark one of the highest elevations in the province. Long ago, when glaciers locked the prairies under a veneer of ice, the Cypress Hills were above this frost, basking under the prehistoric sun. While Canada was crushed under the ice sheet, here

Saskatchewan border crossing

plants and animals survived and evolved into rare strains. Today, campers in Cypress Hills Provincial Park share the land with unusual forms of ferns and strange lizards that, in a gruesome defence tactic, shoot blood from their eyes. The Cypress Hills have long been a place of refuge for man and animal. Chief Sitting Bull and five thousand of his followers sought sanctuary here from vengeful U.S. Cavalry troops more than a century ago. The region also sheltered the last wild bison, plains grizzlies and wolves, and today harbours endangered species such as the trumpeter swan.

Only by driving across Saskatchewan, can one grasp the expanse of the prairie. It is an area of great flatness, land like sea, and a wide sky of pale blue light. Something about the landscape, the geometric fields and the farmhouses hints at uprightness, bible-reading and close-mouthed determination. The road runs straight to the horizon and the highest — often the only — object seen on the landscape is a grain elevator standing guard over the plain.

Still the highway runs on. For countless hours the road dissolves into the haze. You begin to believe there is no landscape here. Although it requires an unusual sort of concentration, driving becomes simple. You point the vehicle toward the horizon and settle back into a somnolent peace, occasionally waking to pass a slow-moving camper. Now and then, the landscape is broken by the shadow of a huge boulder, laid down by retreating glaciers that gouged out the great plains thousands of years ago. The boulders have been polished smooth over the centuries, by bison and cattle happy to find something to rub their hides against.

Saskatchewan was the first province to complete its segment of the Trans-Canada. More than twenty-five years later, certain portions of the road have so many years of asphalt patching that they show a quilt pattern, similar to the patchwork of mixed-farm fields. As for divided highway, Saskatchewan is the leader there too. About half of the road is divided and the four lane segment between Moose Jaw and Regina has been divided for twenty of the Trans-Canada's twenty-five years.

Some things have not changed over the quarter-century since the highway officially opened. Drivers here still wave to oncoming traffic. At one point in eastern Saskatchewan, I counted five out of six drivers who waved. I could imagine only two possible reasons for this phenomenon: I was driving what looked like a local resident's vehicle; or the people in this part of the country were particularly friendly. I liked to think it was the latter. Perhaps because of the friendly drivers I began to enjoy the unchanging landscape, and it surprised me that I was happy in a place where there were no trees. None at all. But the open spaces allowed nature to produce colours that were picturesque but practically unphotographable. Saskatchewan's landscape was stunningly, and only sometimes beautifully, empty.

Oil business is big business in Saskatchewan. In a large expanse along the Trans-Canada near Gull Lake the fields are studded with pump jacks, drawing petroleum from pools thousands of metres below the surface.

Saskatchewan's freshwater lakes and pools are sometimes strange. Perfectly rectangular ponds can be seen at various spots alongside the road. These sloughs, dating back to the construction of the Highway, are called "borrow pits," and were dug to provide road-building material. The dugouts remain as farm water storage areas and, consequently, a habitat for prairie waterfowl.

East of Swift Current, flat lakes can be seen with immaculate white beaches around them. Annual evaporation here exceeds rainfall, and the lakesides are surrounded by alkali soil and salt that is left behind when lakewater, lacking natural drainage, evaporates. At the town of Chaplin, white salts are piled up at one end of Lake Chaplin. Looking like a mountain of snow, this is a massive pile of sodium sulphate reserves. (Sodium sulphate is used mainly in the kraft pulp industry, the glass industry and detergent preparation.)

Lake Chaplin's brine is at its highest density during the hot summer months. But even though the lake's salinity is high, life exists here. Tiny brine shrimp float in the salty water and can be harvested (up to 4,500 kilograms in a day) for hatchery and pet food use.

Saskatchewan's landscape may be austere, but its place names are fantastic. Signs direct wayfarers to the towns of Valjean, Beverly, Eyebrow, Shamrock, Red Jacket, Pense, Percival, Indian Head and Avonlea. Avonlea traces its name to Lucy Maude Montgomery and her popular *Anne of Green Gables* sequel, *Anne of Avonlea*. Montgomery's relatives lived here during homesteading days.

Their names may be comical or romantic but the story of these towns is often sad. Many of southern Saskatchewan's smaller hamlets have died, thanks to the Trans-Canada Highway. More than a hundred years ago, a time when even short distances were an ordeal for rural travel, the Canadian Pacific Railway neatly spread Saskatchewan's towns at sixteen-kilometre intervals. The Trans-Canada changed the face of transportation here and, among other things, eliminated the need for stores and services every sixteen kilometres. Thirty years after the Trans-Canada was pushed through, the ubiquitous grain elevator remains as the only viable business in many communities.

Nearing the industrial centre of Moose Jaw, jet streams cross overhead, streaking the wide expanse of clear blue sky. Moose Jaw is the home of the Canadian air force Snowbirds precision flying team. The team's jets cross the skies above Moose Jaw, practising maneuvers of amazing complexity.

The great grain fields of central Saskatchewan, east of Moose Jaw, cover prehistoric Lake Regina. Underlying the wheatfields and small houses built close to the ground are metres of glacial deposit, covering solid bedrock. When the first settlers arrived on the newly-constructed railway in 1882, the plains were dominated by grasses such as western porcupine grass, wheat grasses and blue grama grass. Over thousands of years, these grasses had converted the lake clay into rich, dark-brown soils that are the soul of Saskatchewan's bountiful agriculture.

Tens of millions of bison once roamed this land, as did the ancestors of the pronghorn antelope that still graze southwestern Saskatchewan's short-grass regions. The prairie wolves and plains grizzlies hunted the region until they were driven to the distant Cypress Hills, where they took a feeble last stand before extinction. Today, a Trans-Canada voyager can hope to spot Richardson's ground squirrels (gophers by the millions!) a coyote, or a leaping jackrabbit.

From a distance Regina looks lovely and familiar. In the fall the city is partly obscured by a haze of grain dust suspended in the air. The dust also causes enlarged, ruddy images of harvest and hunter's moons, and makes it all look mysterious and interesting. Generations ago, this dust was thrown up by threshing machines. Now expensive machines that "combine" grain gathering and the separating of kernels from chaff into one operation harvest the wheat.

In 1882, Regina began as a tiny settlement near what was known as Pile of Bones Creek. The majority of the community's residents were officers of the North-West Mounted Police, sworn to "maintain the right." Some citizens were more difficult to maintain than others. One was Louis Riel.

Although Riel is now considered a hero-martyr of

Lunch Break: Scott Arue, grass cutter near Summerberry, Saskatchewan

Manitoba's history, in 1885 central Canada and Saskatchewan's settlers looked less favourably on the dissident and his Métis followers. After the famous bloody battle and surrender of the Métis at Batoche, Riel was brought to Regina's N.W.M.P. barracks for trial. An all-white, all-English jury found the Métis leader guilty of treason, but recommended mercy. (To other pleas for pardon, Sir John A. MacDonald reputedly answered, "Riel shall hang — though every dog in Quebec bark in his favour.")

Riel mounted the scaffold at the North-West Mounted Police barracks in Regina on November 16, 1885. With his execution, the Métis rebellion — the last armed conflict on Canadian soil — was over.

On the gallows site where Riel was hanged for treason is the modern R.C.M.P. museum. Here, the handcuffs and gun holster worn by Riel, his bible and crucifix, and other memorabilia of the mostly peaceful history of the Mounties, are displayed. In the Training Centre camp next door, Mounted Police recruits undergo six month basic training before being sent to further duties across the country.

The Trans-Canada bypasses most of Regina, carrying traffic to the south and east, and providing just a brief glimpse of the modern and architecturally innovative University of Regina campus.

Prairie grasses, growing at the roadside in eastern Saskatchewan, once provide the sod that was used for settler's homes. Today, the government considers roadside hay a nuisance and dispatches county workers to cut the stuff. I met one of the cutters at the side of the highway, near the hamlet of Summerberry. The fall sun was still warm; the air was fragrant with the smell of freshly-cut grasses. Over a roadside sandwich and coffee we discussed the subject most strangers naturally take up — the weather. He was grateful for the sun and warm air, complaining that usually the boss had them working in open tractors well after the snow began to fall. Sure enough, retracing my path more than a month later, I saw another county worker cutting roadside grasses as the snow whirled around his tractor wheels.

At the town of Indian Head, Saskatchewan

Saskatchewan's universal symbol is the slope-shouldered grain elevator. Clustered every few kilometres along the transcontinental railway tracks, these prairie sentinels are in operation by the hundreds, across the west. I stopped at a Saskatchewan Wheat Pool elevator and talked the agent into giving me a tour. He was obliging enough, but all through the tour I got the feeling that he couldn't understand why someone would be so interested in grain elevator activities. Or was it that he couldn't believe someone could be so dumb as to not know how a grain elevator works?

From the Trans-Canada, Whitewood appears similar to countless towns perched by the side of the C.P.R. tracks. Actually, this peaceful, rural scene hides an aristocratic past. The area's aspen parkland was so reminiscent of European landscapes that a group of French noblemen settled here in 1884. The French aristocrats — the Comte de Soras, Comte de Jumilhac, Comte de Beaudrap and Comte de Langle — dominated Whitewood society during those early years. The counts brought with them gardeners, grooms and servants. Carriages, champagne and thoroughbred horses were regularly imported from France, and ladies wearing the latest gowns from Paris could be seen on Whitewood's streets.

The counts took it upon themselves to bring agricultural industry to eastern Saskatchewan. They inaugurated sugar beet processing, chicory canning and cheese manufacturing. Most of the enterprises failed. What was left of the aristocratic estates was packed up before the turn of the twentieth century, and dispatched to France. Today, the only reminders of the noblemen of Whitewood are the town's French street names.

The Saskatchewan-Manitoba border is a short twenty kilometres east, at the town of Moosmin. Unlike most Saskatchewan hamlets, Moosmin takes full advantage of Trans-Canada Highway traffic. The town is spread along a thin line on both sides of the national highway. Service stations, motels, restaurants, shops — all heartily encourage travellers to stop and rest, before continuing toward the plains and valleys of Manitoba.

MANITOBA

Trans-Canada Highway sign near Winnipeg, Manitoba

Manitoba marks the beginning of Canada's real west. Even though the province saw waves of immigrant settlers long before the rest of Rupert's Land and the Northwest Territories (as western Canada was called then), Manitoba remained a mosaic of distinctive cultures long after younger provinces became more homogenized.

Beyond the Manitoba border, stands of aspen trees grow in thick concentration around green meadows; they patiently wait for farmers to give up the fight, allowing the trees to reclaim land that was once theirs alone. Aspens also stand guard over the Trans-Canada Highway, the sun gilding their green leaves and striking through car windshields. Stapled to a roadside tree, I saw a sign advertising Bubba's Laundromat and Barber Shop at Elkhorn, one of the westernmost towns in Manitoba. I would have stopped for a shave and a tumble dry but Bubba was closed.

The Trans-Canada Highway was built for much more than tourist traffic, as is shown by the number of heavy trucks along the route. And while they may not be as common as roadside gas stations, provincial truck weigh stations are frequently encountered along the route.

After passing dozens of such weigh stations, curiosity got the best of me. I pulled into a Manitoba government station to find out how to weigh a truck. Inside the tiny building, were restrooms, a pay telephone, a brochure rack and a Department of Transport weigh station officer, who quickly got rid of me once he discovered I wanted information, not a toilet or telephone.

Oil and saltwater pumps, seen from the roadside near Virden, are reminders of the briny origin of western Canada. One hundred thirty-six million years ago, the Trans-Canada roadbed was under half a kilometre of water. Today, prehistoric remnants of oil and salt water (the water is pumped back into wells to increase underground pressure and push up oil reserves) are the raw materials of Manitoba's small petroleum industry.

In western Manitoba, the Assiniboine River winds back and forth across the Trans-Canada's path. Near one of these crossings lies Brandon, calling itself the "Wheat City" since in the 1880s it was reputed to lead the world in delivery of grain from farmer's wagons. Views of Brandon from the Trans-Canada are practically impossible, as the townsite lies beyond a rise to the south of the road. However, travellers are greeted in genuine Brandon style at Harry's Ukrainian Kitchen Family Restaurant. This big restaurant offers huge meals and open arm hospitality. My waitress was so effusive that I thought she was going to give me a hug and a kiss for dessert.

Manitoba's · past is evident in its place names. MacGregor hints of the province's first settlers — Irish and Scots who came here under the sponsorship of Douglas, the Earl of Selkirk. St. Eustache recalls the French voyageurs who paddled Manitoba's waterways in search of fur and fortune. Other town names salute Manitoba's largest surge of immigrants, from eastern Europe, who were attracted by the Canadian government promises of freedom and free land.

While I drove near the Carberry Sand Hills, the sun disappeared and a heavy shower of rain swept across the fields and drenched the landscape. On a solitary line of roadside fence posts, bluebirds took refuge inside weather-beaten boxes. Thousands of bluebird boxes have been placed here by volunteers striving to save the species.

At the approach to Portage la Prairie, where the Trans-Canada joins the Yellow Quill Trail, a marker points south to a cairn commemorating Fort la Reine. At this site, in October 1738, Pierre Gaultier de la Vérendrye, the French explorer of Canada's west, built the fourth and most important of his wilderness outposts. La Vérendrye was the first white man to reach the confluence of the Red and Assiniboine rivers, where Winnipeg now stands. Starting from Montréal in 1731, he followed what was to become the voyageur's route up the Ottawa and Mattawa rivers, across Lake Nipissing and along the French River into Lake Huron. Moving along the north shores of Lake Huron and Lake Superior, he then traced a route to the western plains, by way of Rainy River, Lake of the Woods and the Winnipeg River. Along the way, La Vérendrye established forts and trading posts. He was the first European to descend the Winnipeg River, the first to see Lake Winnipeg, first on the Red, Assiniboine and Saskatchewan rivers and probably the first to cross the great plains to the Missouri. Today, Portage la Prairie's water treatment plant occupies the site of La Vérendrye's Fort la Reine.

At Portage la Prairie, western Canada's two major highways meet: the Trans-Canada, which pushes a southern route through the Rockies, and the Yellowhead Highway, connecting the northern communities of Jasper, Edmonton and Saskatoon with Winnipeg, about seventy kilometres farther east. This dual highway crosses the old White Horse Plain (named for a white stallion that, avoiding all attempts at capture, roamed these plains two hundred years ago). At one time this was Métis country and the starting point for their great bison hunts. Once, bison were so great in numbers that no one could have possibly imagined a time when they would not be here.

When Canada was still young, it closed one of the finest real estate deals in history. For the sum of £300,000 (a current price of about one-fifth of a cent per hectare), Canada bought the seven and one half million square kilometre, Rupert's Land and North-Western Territory, from the Hudson's Bay Company. Over time, Canada carved this parcel into the provinces of Manitoba, Alberta and Saskatchewan, with enough left over for the Yukon and Northwest Territories, as well as much of present-day Quebec and Ontario.

In the 1870s, Canada's first priority was to populate these vast, new expanses, in order to assert sovereignty over the west. A series of pamphlets, printed in twenty languages and distributed throughout Europe, called for immigrants to the New World. When they came, in search of the free sixty-five hectare homestead promised by the government of Canada, they inevitably passed through the gateway to the west — Winnipeg.

Winnipeg was first settled by Selkirk's Scottish and Irish homesteaders in 1812. From the 1870s to about 1910, the city saw tens of thousands of immigrants making their way west. Many pioneers liked what they saw or simply ran out of steam early and settled there. The waves of immigrants swelled Winnipeg's population to, for a time, the third largest in the country.

Other cities may shuttle Trans-Canada Highway traffic away from downtown but here the highway runs into the heart of town on Portage Avenue. The route cuts down Broadway Avenue toward Manitoba's Legislative Building. Far beneath a soaring neoclassical dome in a place called the "Pool of the Black Star" I discovered (at the Winnipeg Sketch Club's annual exhibition) misty waterfalls, crows in a stubbled field, exuberant Ukranian dancers and watercolour artist Bianca Sagoo.

Sagoo was born in Italy and, over the years, lived in London, Paris, Kenya and Uganda. Like many immigrants, she came here "only temporarily," but stayed because "once you settle in Winnipeg it's hard to leave." I asked about the city's reputation as a cultural centre and she said, "For some reason, people from many cultures have come to this place and stayed where the climate and the wind and the bugs are terrible. People need to rise above the weather and so they try hard to create a cultural spirit. That's why we have a good ballet, a good playhouse and a great opera."

A few streets beyond the legislature, almost hidden behind advertising signs, is Winnipeg's most historic site — the single remaining gate to the Hudson Bay Company's Upper Fort Gary. In a small park the 1822 gate stands, defying the onslaught of modern buildings. The confluence of the Red River and Assiniboine River was the site of frontier palisades from the mid-eighteenth century. La Vérendrye's men erected Fort Rouge near here in 1738, and the North-West Company's Fort Gibraltar was constructed in the area in 1805. Not well-marked by direction signs, the tiny park is worthy of more recognition.

Past the junction of the rivers, the Trans-Canada

passes through Gallic Winnipeg. Now placards above shops, schools and churches are in French. Nearby is the Winnipeg Mint, where automated assembly lines punch out coins of this and a dozen other countries. Soon the highway joins with its speedier bypass, and heads across eastern Manitoba, toward the Canadian Shield. Winnipeg's boast that it guards the geographical heart of the nation is not far off the mark. Just west of the city a roadsign marks the longitudinal centre of Canada.

In the smoky distance I saw the town of Ste-Anne-des-Chênes. This is the site where the first Métis rebellion, in 1870, was sparked because of a conflict between central Canadian surveyors and local settlers. This rebellion was the primary cause of Manitoba attaining provincial status, that year. Referring to his work at Ste-Anne-des-Chênes, Louis Riel remarked at his trial in 1885 "I know that through the grace of God I am the founder of Manitoba."

Richer is a mostly French-speaking town that, for some reason, changed its name from Coteau-de-Chêne. Richer is also geologically important. Here the prairie abruptly ends at the "wall," the great mass of the Canadian Shield. At a perfect dividing line, the plains and fields give way to stands of aspen, birch and evergreen trees.

Soon the route passes West Hawk Lake (created when a meteor smashed into Manitoba) and approaches the Ontario boundary. For more than a thousand kilometres, the Trans-Canada will wind through the Shield, a landscape that appears much the same as it did when the glaciers receded tens of thousands of years ago.

Cold, foggy morning near Richer, Manitoba

Opposite page
Roger's Pass, British Columbia — from above! **John Devaney**

Silver Highway
Photo Contest Winner
Trans-Canada Highway east of Winnipeg, **Dave Reede**

Toos Vanderhoven, son Marty & Salt
the cat near fruitstand at Warren,
Ontario

Banff National Park, Alberta

Following page
Ranch cat, Alberta, **Dr. Van E. Christou**

Thunderbird Park, Victoria, British Columbia

Thunderbird Park, Victoria, British Columbia

Hell's Gate, Fraser Canyon, British Columbia

Following page
Tree in ice storm near Calgary, Alberta, **Stan Kruk**

Horseshoe Bay and B.C. Ferries docks,
British Columbia mainland

Horseshoe Bay and B.C. Ferries docks,
British Columbia mainland

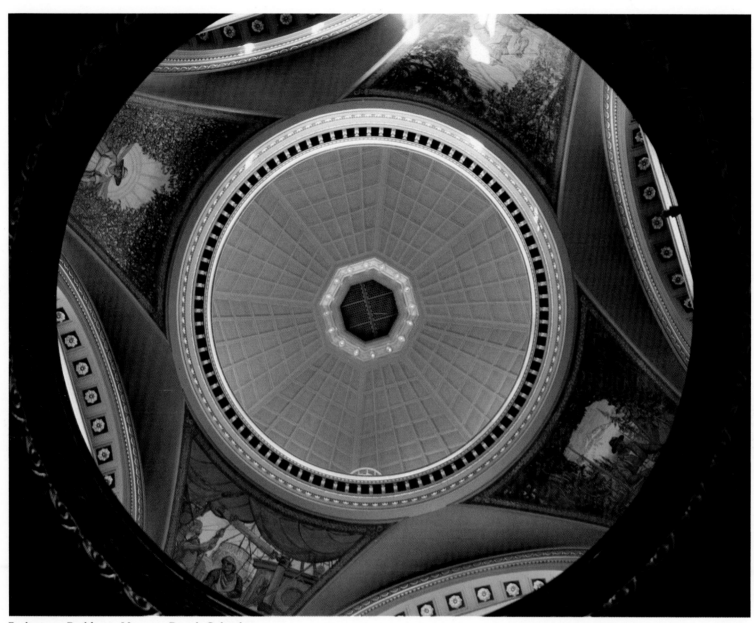

Parliament Buildings, Victoria, British Columbia

Notre Dame de Bonsecours, Vieux Montréal, Quebec

Following page
Steve Fonyo — Trans-Canada
Highway near Victoria, British
Columbia, **Bob Crosby**

Landscape near Ashcroft, British Columbia

View from Mile "0", Beacon Hill Park, Victoria, British Columbia

Following page
Silver Highway
Photo Contest Winner
Snow fence, Alberta, **Stan Kruk**

Sunrise, Northern Ontario, **John Devaney**

Radio model airplane club next to Trans-Canada Highway, Sault Ste. Marie, Ontario

Following page
Frog, *swamp near Gananoque, Ontario*
D. Lorente

ONTARIO

Ontario, the province that has more money, people, urban areas and industry than any other, also has the longest stretch of the Trans-Canada Highway. There are two Trans-Canada paths through the province: the Ottawa Valley route, which follows the old voyageur trail up the Ottawa River, and a Central Ontario route which goes south along Georgian Bay to Orillia, then moves northeast through Peterborough to connect with the northern Trans-Canada just west of Ottawa.

Travelling east on Highway 17, the first major body of water is Lake of the Woods, which contains more than 14,000 islands and is surrounded by evergreens. (The area was misnamed. The natives correctly called it "Lake of the Islands.") On the lake, waves were blue-black and froth was being whipped from their crests. The landscape had changed and I found I liked this new sense of wilderness.

Past numerous fishing and hunting resorts, Kenora, the first community of note on the highway, is marked by a giant fish statue named "Huskie the Muskie." "Kenora" sounds like a lovely Indian name. In fact, the word is an acronym for the three separate communities which were here at the turn of the century — *Ke*ewatin, *Nor*man and *Rat* Portage. So much for romanticism.

Although the landscape is wild, the Trans-Canada roadside is lined with billboards shouting "Minnows, Worms and Leeches For Sale," "Granny's Rock Shop is OPEN. Sound yer' horn and Granny will come runnin'," "Welcome to Big, Beautiful Batchawana Bay" and "The health inspector eats here and drinks the water!" Thanks to the TCH, advertising has come to the north.

The track through northern Ontario and the lakehead region is rugged; the highway winds through corridors of blasted-out rock cliffs and passes by boggy lakes and muskeg. Flys and mosquitoes torment roadcrew workers each summer when they repair the winter's road damage. Whiskey jacks (Canada jays) fly around red and jack pine trees, stealing food from the tourists' picnic baskets.

Here, in and around towns with names like Wabigoon and Dinorwic, is the edge of Ontario's remote north, where people still make their living on trap lines. Beaver, martin, fisher and other furbearing animals are trapped today using methods that differ only slightly from those used centuries ago.

Close to Dryden, I stopped at Rose's Bake Shop. At a kitchen table in the roadside house I ate award-winning apple pie and listened to Rose explain why she opened her house to strangers. "This way," she said, "I always have someone to talk to . . . otherwise I'd never see anybody around here. Not enough neighbours."

The town of Dryden has its Trans-Canada mascot

Trans-Canada Highway midpoint, Chippewa Falls, Ontario

— you'd think it was a northern Ontario law to have one — a huge steel and concrete moose known as "Maxmillian." Game is plentiful in this region and some people bag a moose without intending to. Many a vehicle has been totalled in a nighttime collision with a highway-crossing moose. Traffic hazards here come in all forms.

Near the town of Raith nature finally tossed something different my way — Kakabeka (thundering waters) Falls. According to the ancient story, Greenmantle, an Ojibway princess imprisoned by an enemy war party, pretended to guide the captors to her village, but instead guided them over these falls to their deaths.

The Trans-Canada Highway skirts the city of Thunder Bay (until 1970 known as Port Arthur and Fort William) and heads northeast around Lake Superior. For a hundred-kilometre stretch starting at Thunder Bay, the Trans-Canada is known as the Terry Fox Courage Highway, named in honour of the last steps Terry Fox took on his Marathon of Hope, an attempt to run across Canada to support cancer research.

In the 1950s, it was not possible to drive across this part of Canada. Even today, the Trans-Canada connects some of the wildest land in Ontario between Thunder Bay and White River. The Lakehead section of the highway is 1,500 kilometres of rock cliff faces, lake mists and winding road.

The highway passes through White River, known as the coldest town in Ontario. Temperatures in January average about −17° and extremes have been recorded as low as −51°.

For some reason the best-known Trans-Canada Highway sculpture is a giant steel goose at Wawa, Ontario. (Wawa is the Ojibway word for "wild goose," and the area was named because of the Canada Geese that rest on Wawa Lake during migration.) Wawa's roadside mascot was erected on September 17, 1960, to commemorate the completion of the last link of Ontario's Lake Superior Trans-Canada route. During the 1960s this park was crowded with hitchikers looking for the next lift west.

South of Wawa, the highway passes through Lake Superior Provincial Park, a natural wilderness area stretching more than fifty kilometres along the lake's eastern shore. A short access road west of the highway leads to Agawa Rock. Scattered about the base of this thirty-metre rock are thirty-five Indian pictographs, said to illustrate the story of a war party that destroyed an enemy village here 150 years ago. A huge vertical gash defaces Agawa Rock. Modern scientists believe it resulted from the erosion of a narrow joint, but the Indians have a more concise explanation for the break — this was the path of descent of the devil Manabozko.

At the edge of Lake Superior Provincial Park the town of Montreal Harbour marks what was, prior to the completion of the Trans-Canada Highway, the northern terminus of Ontario Highway 17. Less than thirty years ago, communities north of here were accessible only by water or rail. Montreal Harbour is also the heart of Group of Seven country. The painters travelled here by train in the 1920s.

Southward, Chippewa Falls marks an important site on the Trans-Canada route. A roadside cairn says, "This plaque stands at the half-way point of the Trans-Canada Highway, which runs from Saint John's Newfoundland to Victoria, British Columbia. The highway's construction, in conjunction with the provinces, was authorized by the federal parliament in 1949. The official opening for through traffic of this 4,860-mile route, of which about 1,453 miles are within Ontario, took place on September 3, 1962. However with the completion of a section of Highway 11 between Longlac and Hearst in 1944 it had been possible previously to cross Ontario from Quebec to Manitoba. The opening of the Trans-Canada Highway provided a shorter, first-class route drawing together widely separated regions of Ontario." The monument was erected by the Ontario Motor League in memory of Doctor Perry E. Dolittle, father of the Trans-Canada Highway.

Sault Ste Marie faces the Michigan city of the same name, across the St Mary's River. For more than two hundred years the settlement was an important fur trading post. The French established a military post

Sudbury, Ontario

at the sault (rapids) in 1750 and the British took possession of the fort a dozen years later.

East of the Soo the landscape opens. Sheer rock faces are replaced by farm plots and, in the distance, the trees of northern Ontario's bush country. A town called Espanola commemorates the first white inhabitant — an unknown slave woman. The Ojibway captured the woman during one of their raids far to the south. The Spanish captive was brought back to the north shore of Lake Huron and lived the rest of her life there. When French explorers came in contact with the Ojibway community, their vocabulary was peppered with Spanish words.

At Sudbury, the Trans-Canada splits into its Ottawa Valley and Central Ontario routes. Highway 69 heads south along Georgian Bay through Parry Sound and Huronia. At the Martyr's Shrine, memorials recall Jesuit martyrs: Jean de Brébeuf, Gabriel Lalement and eight others who suffered incredible tortures before being burned at the stake by several hundred Iroquois warriors.

Near the town of Waubaushene, the highway turns east toward Orillia. Stephen Leacock's Sunshine Sketches of a Little Town was a popular, thinly disguised satire, filled with descriptions of the sights, sounds and citizens of Orillia. The town today remembers the humourist at the Stephen Leacock Memorial Home.

East of Orillia, the Trans-Canada covers four hundred kilometres, around Lake Simcoe, past Peter-

Big Nickel, Sudbury, Ontario

borough, the Trent Canal, Perth's dairylands and on to Ottawa. Edwardian farmhouses are common throughout the journey, their solid red brick faces decorated with clean, white wood porches sporting fretwork trim.

Back up north, the air has been clean enough to make porch-sitting a popular pastime. Sudbury's symbol, a giant nickel, overlooks the junction of Highway 69 and the northern Trans-Canada segment, Highway 17. The symbol is appropriate; Sudbury is home to, among others, the Creighton Mine, largest nickel mine in the world. Here smokestacks rise nearly four hundred metres.

At one time, when the Sudbury area supplied more than ninety percent of the world's refined nickel, sulphurous emissions seared the landscape barren, and American astronauts trained here for their moon walks. In later years, tough world competition cut Canada's share of the market to well below fifty percent, leaving Sudbury with tens of thousands of unemployed. Today, Sudbury has cleaned up her act and the city is a better place to live.

Although great strides have been made by Sudbury's mining companies to eliminate the adverse affects of their industry, the landscape remains bleak and bumpy. The devastation of earlier years can still be seen, though once-barren rock faces now sprout trees and small bushes. Sudbury's environs remain a completely man-made landscape, a deliberate monstrosity of defilement. It will take decades to restore a land that was destroyed by only a few years of indiscriminate mining and refining.

At Coniston, the mined land is desolate and unreclaimed. At the turn of the century, mining techniques here and in nearby Sudbury included heap-roasting raw ore to process out the pure minerals. Giant outdoor bonfires destroyed the landscape in many ways. Initially massive amounts of timber were downed to supply the day-and-night fires. The removal of the timber exposed the ground to erosion. The roast spewed enormous amounts of sulphur dioxide fumes, killing the remaining trees and vegetation in a wide surrounding area. The damage was complete by 1920 and even today the Coniston area is scarred and empty. There is no greenery here. The view is hard and grey, the rocky land split, wrinkled and torn open.

North Bay is famous for babies. Nearby, in 1934, the Dionne quintuplets were born. The Dionne Homestead Museum, moved from its original location in the nearby town of Callander, is located at the Trans-Canada roadside next to a visitor information centre. Inside are displays on anything anyone would ever want to know about this most prolific family.

East of North Bay I stopped at a spot where the waters of a pond lapped against the highway. The head of this pond is where La Vase Portages began, three canoe portages connecting Trout Lake and the lower La Vasse River. The voyageurs came here along a water and portage trail that started at Rivière-du-Loup and carried the explorers, missionaries and fur traders along the St. Lawrence, up the Ottawa and Mattawa rivers, across to Lake Nipissing and the French River, into Lake Huron, across what is now the Sault Canal and along the shores of Lake Superior. From the seventeenth to the nineteenth century, this pond carried the boats of Etienne Brûlé, Champlain, Brébeuf, La Vérendrye and Alexander MacKenzie.

East of Mattawa, the Trans-Canada approaches the Ottawa River. For more than three hundred kilometres the highway follows the Ottawa Valley, past signs clocking distance to the nation's capital. Along this track are communities transformed by the military during World War II, and then by Atomic Energy of Canada Limited. At the Chalk River laboratories, Canadians scientists developed the cobalt bomb, used to kill cancer. Close by at Petawawa, a landscape of rolling sand dunes is still used by the Canadian armed forces as a training ground for tank warfare. Roadside signs warn drivers of tanks and armoured cars approaching — one of the Trans-Canada Highway's more unusual hazards.

Just west of Ottawa, Highway 17 becomes Highway 417, the Queensway freeway that shoots through Ottawa. A kilometre to the north are Parliament Hill and the buildings of the federal government. Ottawa is Canada's capital because Queen Victoria became bored with Quebec City, Toronto, Kingston and

Stanley Park, Vancouver, British Columbia

Montreal fighting over the designation. She poked her finger at a spot on the map, roughly halfway between Montreal and Toronto, and declared that the hamlet of Bytown was to be the government seat. The locals hastily changed the name to Ottawa thinking this was a nicer sounding name. The year was 1857. Toronto's Goldwyn Smith described Ottawa as a "sub-arctic lumber village converted by royal mandate into a political cockpit," and the American press quipped that the choice was wise, as Ottawa could not be captured by invaders because they would become lost in the woods trying to find it. The few Canadians interested in politics at the time dubbed her "Westminster in the Wilderness," but the arguments against Ottawa were dampened when, two years later, construction of the parliament buildings began. By then, any change of heart was too costly to consider.

Ottawa today is a city of parks, tree-lined driveways, tulips and government offices. Two of Ottawa's national museums are within sight of the Trans-Canada Highway, at the Victoria Memorial Museum.

The roar of Queensway traffic is dampened by stately trees surrounding the ramparts of the museum. Inside, where the leaders of the country once sparred in parliamentary debate, are the skeletons of mammoth dinosaurs and the dusty furniture of a Depression prairie kitchen. The complex is home to the National Museum of Natural Sciences and the Canadian Museum of Civilization.

The Victoria Memorial Museum was built in 1905 and, with bureaucratic haste, by 1911 a few natural science exhibits were open to the public. The country's first dinosaur enhibit was complete by 1913. But within three years, a fire in downtown Ottawa caused the building to be used for a greater national purpose.

A disastrous fire swept across Parliament Hill in 1916, destroying virtually all of the centre block. Searching for somewhere to hold parliamentary sessions, the prime minister's eyes fell on the Victoria Memorial Museum. Within days, museum collections were shoved aside and, for four years, parliament sat in the museum's auditorium. Members complained about paleontologists working on fossils in the basement. One minister insisted that the fleas and lice that infested the building were from the three-million-year-old animals downstairs. After more than seventy-five years, the museum's best displays are still the dinosaur skeleton reconstructions — including the original skeleton first displayed in 1913.

The natural history exhibits are juxtaposed with re-creations of human history. Probably the most compelling display is a collection of Iroquois masks used in healing rituals. Because the masks are carved from a living tree, they, in the Iroquois beliefs, remain alive. The Iroquois come to the museum each year and conduct a ceremony, which includes feeding the masks a corn mush, to keep the faces in good spirits.

The Queensway passes over the Rideau Canal where joggers and cyclists exercise on waterside paths in summer and ice skaters glide along the canal in winter. Within minutes, the buildings of the world's coldest capital dissolve into rich farmland and the Trans-Canada branches off, continuing eastward through Ontario's French-speaking communities (many with incongruous English names like Wendover, Alfred and Hawkesbury) to the Quebec border.

QUEBEC

Where the Trans-Canada Highway crosses the Quebec boundary, highway numbers change from Ontario 417 to Quebec autoroute 40. The Ottawa Valley landscape remains the same, as does the predominance of French communities. The official name of the road is now "Autoroute transcanadienne."

Europe's explorers came to Canada in search of greater glory for God, man and monarch. As far back as 1496, John Cabot sailed to Canada with letters patent from Henry VII that empowered him to "seeke out, discover and finde whatsoever isles, countrey's, regions or provinces of the heathen and infidels wheresoever they be, which before this time have been unknown to all Christians."

In 1535, Jacques Cartier became the first European to explore the Gulf of St. Lawrence and follow its river inland. Cartier was under the impression that his course would lead to the Orient, but he was turned back at the Lachine Rapids. The land Cartier found did not yield pepper but it did supply a bounty of fur, minerals and timber. More importantly, he established contact with the people of two Iroquois, communities of note: Stadacona and Hochelaga.

The man most closely associated with New France was Samuel de Champlain, royal geographer of the French court. In 1608, Champlain followed Cartier's path and, near Stadacona, established a post where the narrowing St. Lawrence is guarded by the bulk of Cape Diamond. His men constructed a rude wooden fort that became the foundation of Quebec City. Thirty, four years later the Sieur de Maisonneuve and Jeanne Mance established a mission some 250 kilometres upstream at Hochelaga, on an island crowned by a mountain of volcanic rock that Jacques Cartier had christened Mount Royal. The western approach to Montreal travels past industrial plants that employ a good portion of the area's residents. After many kilometres of industry, at the confluence of the Ottawa and St. Lawrence Rivers, freeway signs point to Centre Ville. Here the peak of Mount Royal and the dome of St. Joseph's Oratory rise into view.

Near Mount Royal Park is Montreal's famed church of healing, St. Joseph's Oratory, with its dome soaring higher than even Maisonneuve's Mount Royal cross. The oratory exists because of Brother André. In 1904, Brother André built a small wooden chapel on the west slope of Mount Royal to honour Saint Joseph. He treated the sick in this church and preached that devotion to Saint Joseph would relieve human suffering. The sick came and many were healed, leaving behind their crutches and wheelchairs to attest to the cures. The tiny chapel still stands, but is now dominated by an enormous basilica. Pilgrims visit the church and shrine, some of them climbing the oratory's steep steps on their knees. The crutches left behind by the healed cover

walls along a long hallway, and in the room where Saint Brother André's tomb lies the devout reverently lay hands on his sarcophagus, drawing out the brother's healing powers. In the basilica, a priest stands near the high altar, directing his congregation in song. The grand organ's tones boom and rumble over the congregation.

It takes time to drive out of Montreal. Beyond the maze of freeways and bridges funneling a torrent of traffic, the gray outlines of apartment and office towers and the pavilions of Expo 67, La Ronde and Olympic Park give way to farmland. The city is replaced by a flat, green landscape dotted with black white cows.

East of Montreal, hugging the American frontier, are Quebec's Eastern Townships, first settled by British immigrants and New England loyalists after the American Revolution. Although the towns today retain Anglo names like Sherbrooke and Drummondville, they are more than ninety percent Francophone.

The countryside looks lovely, with farms and fields of a classic kind: long vistas over the low hills, clapboard houses and smooth fields of browsing sheep and fat cattle. In towns like St. Apollinaire and Kamouraska, the church dominates the townscape; without Mother Church the town would be faceless.

The Trans-Canada route from Montreal to Quebec City passes through townships with farms and fields jammed against the Saint Lawrence. The explorers of New France sailed these waters and paddled into the wilderness, along the way founding riverside colonies. To this day, most of Canada's six million Francophones live in Quebec's two major cities or in the small shoreside towns along the river.

Six hundred kilometres west of its gulf, the St. Lawrence narrows, to form what the Indians call a "kebek." Here, the river's north bank rises a hundred metres to the peak of Cape Diamond. Samuel de Champlain recognized this rock as a perfect spot for lookouts scanning downstream; from here a solidly braced gun could control all approaches. On viewing Cape Diamond in 1608, Champlain declared, "Upon this rock I will build my city." A fledging colony, fortifications, and the city of Quebec did grow on the rock. A hundred fifty years later, the British mounted the cliff and, on the Plains of Abraham, captured the city.

The Trans-Canada Highway, by-passes Quebec City. As I passed by Lévis, where Wolfe's guns blasted at the fortress of Quebec in 1759, I saw mist swirling about the ancient capital's ramparts across the narrows. If any city was worth a short detour off the Trans-Canada, this was it.

I liked Quebec City immediately. It was grand without being grandoise. I liked the look of the stone houses and cobblestone streets of the old city. Even though I was told the weather here is far from perfect, I thought: I could live here.

Between the St. Lawrence and Quebec's fortifications, are the seventeenth century stone houses of Lower Town. A precipitous staircase, called the *Casse-Cou* (the break-neck stairs) leads from the ancient ramparts to the cobblestone streets below. Lower Town's walls, a rock face lined with guns and houses worn with age, conjure images of a time past.

Even with your mind firmly in the present, it's easy to get lost in Quebec City's narrow, twisting, semi-vertical streets. No matter, the senses are rewarded at every turn, even if it's a wrong one. Today Lower Town's streets are filled with excellent cafés, bars and shops.

Above the battlements and fortifications is the century-old Château Frontenac, commanding high ground above the old town and river. A prime example of Canadian railway architecture, it was built in medieval French style in 1893, with numerous turrets and verdigris copper roofs.

When the British besieged Quebec, this was the site of the Governor's residence. For generations, the remains of this vice-regal residence were covered by the boardwalk planks of Dufferin Terrace, built on a cliff edge above the St. Lawrence. More recently, Parks Canada archaeologists ripped away the planks and found a treasure trove of Quebec history. The chief archaeologist at the site told me, "As an historic

Lower Town, Quebec City

archaeological site, this is one of the greatest locations in the country. There is a great deal to be found and a great deal to be understood; eventually, another generation of archaeologists will stand here and realise a global picture of life in Quebec's past times."

Beyond the excavations lie Canada's most famous battefields. The Plains of Abraham saw the culmination of a battle that had gone on for nearly two months in 1759. The British, under the command of thirty-one-year-old James Wolfe, bombarded Quebec City for weeks from Lévis, across the river. On the night of September 12, Wolfe's troops stole up river and landed at Anse au Foulon. By morning they had scaled the heights and were on the Plains of Abraham, in battle position before the city. Unprepared French troops fought bravely under the Marquis de Montcalm, but in twenty minutes Wolfe was dead, Montcalm was mortally wounded and New France was a British possession.

Between 1820 and 1832, the British built above the Plains of Abraham the Citadel, to protect Canada from American attack.

Henry David Thoreau compared the Citadel to Gibraltar's fortifications, when he visited Quebec in 1850. He was given a tour of the Citadel by a young soldier of a Highland regiment. Thoreau wrote later that "He told us he had been here about three years, and had formerly been stationed at Gibaltar. As if his regiment, having perchance been nestled amid the rocks of Edinburgh Castle, must flit from roost to rock thenceforth over the earth's surface, like a bald eagle or other bird or prey, from eyrie to eyrie."

The Citadel is the only fortification in North America still garrisoned by regular troops. The Royal 22nd (the "Van Doos"), the only French-speaking regiment in Canada's armed forces, are the appointed guardians of these walls. A Lieutenant of the regiment escorted me about the four-pointed-star fort, and talked about the Citadel's history.

Back on the Trans-Canada, between Lévis and Rivière-du-Loup, the Laurentians rise to the north. There is a good view of Ile d'Orléans from the highway. The long flat island stays in view for several minutes. Continuously inhabited since the seventeenth century, it was originally named Ile de Bacchus because of wild grapes that grew here. Its farmland is dotted with eighteenth century French churches, mills and homes.

The route northeast of Quebec City, toward the Gaspé Peninsula is one of the most pleasant along the Trans-Canada. But the St. Lawrence Seaway's influence is never far away. One town along the way, L'Islet-sur-Mer, has produced so many renowned mariners for so many centuries that it's known as *la patrie des marins*, "the sailor's homeland." The most famous of these was Joseph-Elzéar Bernier, the man who, on twelve voyages, established Canada's sovereignty over the Arctic archipelago.

Another town, St-Jean Port Joli, is considered Quebec's woodcarving capital. Here, in converted quonset huts and industrial buildings, artisans carve local wood into old men and women. The buildings where the artists work seem uninspiring, but their carvings are so filled with character that the art pieces are snapped up by collectors across the country.

Near Rivière-du-Loup, the Trans-Canada approaches the St. Lawrence. The citizens of Rivière-du-Loup argue about the origin of their town's name. One story connects the title with the sea lions (loup marins) that once frequented the mouth of the river, and another version claims that the name came from the French ship "Le Loup," which was stranded at the mouth of the river in 1660. No matter what the origin, Rivière-du-Loup's eight waterfalls — the largest falling a total of thirty-eight metres — make for a picturesque stop. At Rivière-du-Loup, the road turns south onto Quebec Autoroute 185. A short distance over hilly terrain, past St-Louis-du-Ha-Ha (named, legend says, after an Indian chief), is the start of Atlantic Canada, the province of New Brunswick.

My first, impression of New Brunswick was wonderful. It was a rural province filled with people. On every stretch of Trans-Canada Highway 2 the view includes at least a cottage, a farmhouse and yard or a small community with a white clapboard church. And unlike other parts of the route, where villages lie on access roads a few kilometres beyond, here the towns straddle the Trans-Canada.

New Brunswick's most northern city is Edmundston, French-speaking capital of the Republic of Madawaska. The republic traces its origins from border disputes of the mid-1700s, when Quebec and New Brunswick fought over who would have jurisdiction over the old French seigneury of Madawaska. After decades of wrangling, the Americans joined the foray and demanded the region be annexed to Maine. During the War of 1812, Madawaskans were required to switch allegiance, depending on who had, at that moment, stronger territorial claims. When all the parties finally agreed to declare the area part of New Brunswick in 1842, Madawaskans were fed up enough to begin calling themselves simply "citizens of the Republic of Madawaska." The Brayons of Madwaska still speak with a dialect peculiar to this region.

Visitors to Edmundston receive a free Madawaskan flag, if they care to detour off the Trans-Canada Highway to City Hall. I was granted an audience with the President of the Republic, Edmundston's Mayor J. Pins Bard: he stepped out of his office, said hello, shook my hand and rushed out of the building, commenting that affairs of the republic were calling. The receptionist told me later he was probably on his way to lunch.

The Saint John river comes into view soon after the highway passes Edmundston and moves smoothly along a wide channel. From here to well past Fredericton, the Trans-Canada follows the river; from Edmunston to Grand Falls, it divides nations — east is New Brunswick and Canada, west is Maine and America.

At Hartland, New Brunswick, a thirty second detour takes travellers off the Trans-Canada and over the world's longest covered bridge — stretching 391 metres across the Saint John. At either end of the structure, gift and craft shops squeeze against the roadway. I stopped at one and talked for a while with the proprietress, who never stopped knitting. As for the whys and wherefores of covered bridges, she recited an explanation I'm sure was repeated hundreds of times a day. "In the old days, the bridges were made of wood that was exposed to the rotting effects of sun and rain. The life expectancy of a covered bridge was about eighty years, compared to ten years for an uncovered one. So they covered 'em."

Between Woodstock and Fredericton, two streams join the Saint John River. Inspired by the tongue-twisting names, Dalhousie English Professor James de Mille penned the following lines, more than a hundred years ago:

Sweet maiden of Passamaquoddy,
Shall we seek for communion of souls
Where the deep Mississippi meanders,
Or the distant Saskatchewan rolls?
Ah no! in New Brunswick I'll find thee,
A sweetly sequestered nook,
Where the sweet gliding Skoodawabskookis
Conjoins with the Skoodawabskook . . .
Let others sing loudly of Saco,
Of Quoddy, and Tattamagouche,
Of Kennebeccasis, and Quaco.
Of Merigonishe, and Buctouche.
Of Nashwaak, and Magaguadavique,
Or Memmerimammericook —
There's none like the Skoodawabskookis
Excepting the Skoodawabskook!

The highway leading into Fredericton is a lawn ornament collector's dream. A number of roadside homes have huge displays of gaudily painted ornaments, all for sale at "New Brunswick's best prices." As the Trans-Canada nears the centre of town, it crosses the Saint John River over Princess Margaret Bridge. Near a verdant expanse called "The Green," the spire of Christ Church Cathedral and the dome of the New Brunswick Legislative Buildings rise above their surroundings.

I was made to feel welcome in Fredericton. "Come on in and have some lunch!" It was not until I visited Atlantic Canada that I received this kind of invitation. People struck up conversations with me in any situation — in line at the department store, in a restaurant and on the Green. As soon as the city information bureau counsellor found out I was a visitor, I was given a free parking card to put on my windshield.

Beneath the imposing spire of Christ Church Cathedral, the assistant curate told me the history of the place, taking particular care to emphasize that, constructed between 1845 and 1853, this was the first Anglican church to be built in a new location since the Norman Conquest. He was also proud to say that, roughly 130 years after their creation, frescos decorating Christ Church's chancel walls were cleaned, millimetre by millimetre, using pencil erasers.

Christ Church Cathedral faces the riverside Green. Along a substantial stretch of the Saint John riverside, the Green fronts Victorian homes, protected by a line of stately elm trees. I spoke with a woman who had lived for about six years in one of the most beautifully decorated of these century-old homes. She was less than enthusiastic. Her comment was, "It's all right I guess, but it's not modern! It doesn't have the amenities of

Lawn ornaments near Fredericton, New Brunswick

a new house; with the high ceilings it's hard to heat, the plumbing thumps and bangs . . . this old house gets to me sometimes. But what can I do? My husband loves it — and I don't want to move without him."

The 1882 New Brunswick Legislative Buildings are in the city centre. My tour guide through the place was the Sergeant at Arms of the New Brunswick Legislative Assembly. For more than forty years he had served the province as steward of the mace and keeper of the order in the legislature. This man, who had more important matters to consider, gladly took time to give me a personal tour. His huge set of keys unlocked every door in the building, including that on a glass case holding New Brunswick's ceremonial mace, which the Sergeant is sworn to guard with his authority.

Fredericton is on the site of the Acadian community of St. Anne's Point, an Acadian village dating from around 1733. In 1758, the British swept up the Saint John River burning homes and expelling Acadians. A colony of some two thousand American Loyalists moved up river and settled at St. Anne's Point on October 8, 1783. The winter was harsh and most of the Loyalists, who were forced to endure the severe weather while living in tents, perished. Their cemetery lies near the banks of the Saint John. All that remains today in the Loyalist Cemetery are a couple of crumbling grave markers and a cross honouring the poor.

Rural Canadians that I met along the Trans-Canada were not in the least surprised to hear that I was travelling across the country by road. On the other hand, city dwellers — even those living in smaller cities like Fredericton or Charlottetown, were shocked to hear that anyone would, by choice, drive across Canada from Victoria to St. John's. City residents fly any substantial distances while country dwellers still consider car trips to be the natural way to travel.

If there was any doubt that this is potato and blueberry country, a giant steel potato and a huge concrete blueberry decorate roadside produce stands between Fredericton and Moncton. Further on, the Loyalist Grandfather Clock Company ticks by the side of the Trans-Canada Highway near Gagetown, New Brunswick. No giant clock sits at the side of the road but visitors are welcomed to the factory to watch craftspeople build timepieces using age-old techniques.

The most common building seen between Fredericton and Moncton is the country church. These white clapboard structures stand at regular and frequent intervals along the route. Cut from a similar mold, each church is painted a pristine white and sports a traditional pointed steeple.

The Trans-Canada Highway skirts north of Moncton, but the city tries its best to entice travellers off the road. As a result, Moncton is known for some quirky tourist attractions: Magnetic Hill and the tidal bore. Magnetic Hill is meant to illustrate an optical illusion that any Trans-Canada traveller has already experienced too many times. That is, the car is actually moving downhill when it appears to be moving up, or vice versa. The tidal bore, best seen from Bore Park off Main Street in central Moncton, promises a moving wall of water that plows up the Petitcodiac River as the tide rushes in. Unfortunately, many tourists watch the tidal bore during times of the month when the "wall" of water is an unimpressive few centimetres high.

Southeast of Sackville, an extensive array of red-and-white radio transmitting towers sit on the north side of the Trans-Canada Highway. From these towers, the signals of Radio Canada International are broadcast, in many languages, to points in Europe, Mexico and beyond. The Canadian Broadcasting Corporation's short wave radio service chose to locate the transmitting antennae here to take advantage of the water-saturated marshland which, by improving the electical ground, strengthens radio signals that are bounced off the ionosphere. Near here is the turn-off for Trans-Canada Highway 16 which goes past Port Elgin to the end of the line at Cape Tormentine, New Brunswick.

Near Port Elgin, I passed a hand-painted roadside invitation that I couldn't turn down. The sign said, "Visit Andy's Dummy Farm. 1 mile." A mile along, another sign at the side of the road declared "ANDY'S DUMYS (sic). FUN FOR ALL." Another sign next to it said, "If you didn't come to laugh, we don't want you!" It was here that I met the funniest, most congenial person along the Trans-Canada Highway.

Andy MacDonald's first words when I stepped out of my car were, "You're just the person I've been waiting to see! I'm bored silly walking around here by myself. And I'm not going to say another word until you come inside the house and have something to eat!" Over cheese sandwiches and coffee, I learned that Andy is not a native New Brunswicker — he's from Cape Breton Island — and that he is a best-selling author of Cape Breton Island humour — three books in total.

In a few hours, I learned everything about Andy's life, starting from his childhood: "I was born sixty-nine years ago at Sydney Mines, Cape Breton Island; there was twelve in the family. My pa was a coal miner and very strict. We weren't even allowed to yawn on Sundays. Had to wait till Monday." About his collection of life-size dummies: "I've got over five hundred dummies here. Made 'em all myself and wrote the sayings on 'em. Took nineteen years so far." He continued, "I use plastic bottles for the heads and whatever clothes I can find for the body. Sometimes my wife comes around asking, 'Andy, have you seen my red rubber boots?' And right away I remember what dummy's got them on but I don't tell the wife."

Each of Andy's dummies has a small hand-written sign attached. Taking me on a tour, he explained, "Hell, I like to make people laugh, that's my theory in life. I like to befuddle people's minds!" and he picked out his favourites. "Look at this one here. It says, 'You know this country would be a great place if you could find the Prime Minister a good job.' And this one says, 'My mother-in-law's gettin' well-er every day, dammit'." He pointed out a banana tree (a birch tree with hundreds of plastic bananas tied to its branches), tire trees (forty year old trees growing from the holes inside rubber tires), a "hubba hubba" tree (another birch, this time with hubcaps hanging from its limbs) and more dummies.

As I was leaving, and stopped to take a final shot of the sign at the roadside, Andy explained why the entrance sign spells "dummies" as "DUMYS." He warned, "Don't you tell people I can't spell. Simple fact is, I ran out of room! Wasn't going to waste that good wood sign just because there's no room to spell it right."

A few kilometres past Port Elgin, I reached Cape Tormentine, land's end for the province of New Brunswick. After a one hour ferry crossing, the Trans-Canada Highway continues through Canada's small wonder, Prince Edward Island.

Following page
Christ Church Cathedral, Fredericton, New Brunswick

Andy MacDonald and Andy's dummy farm, Port Elgin, New Brunswick

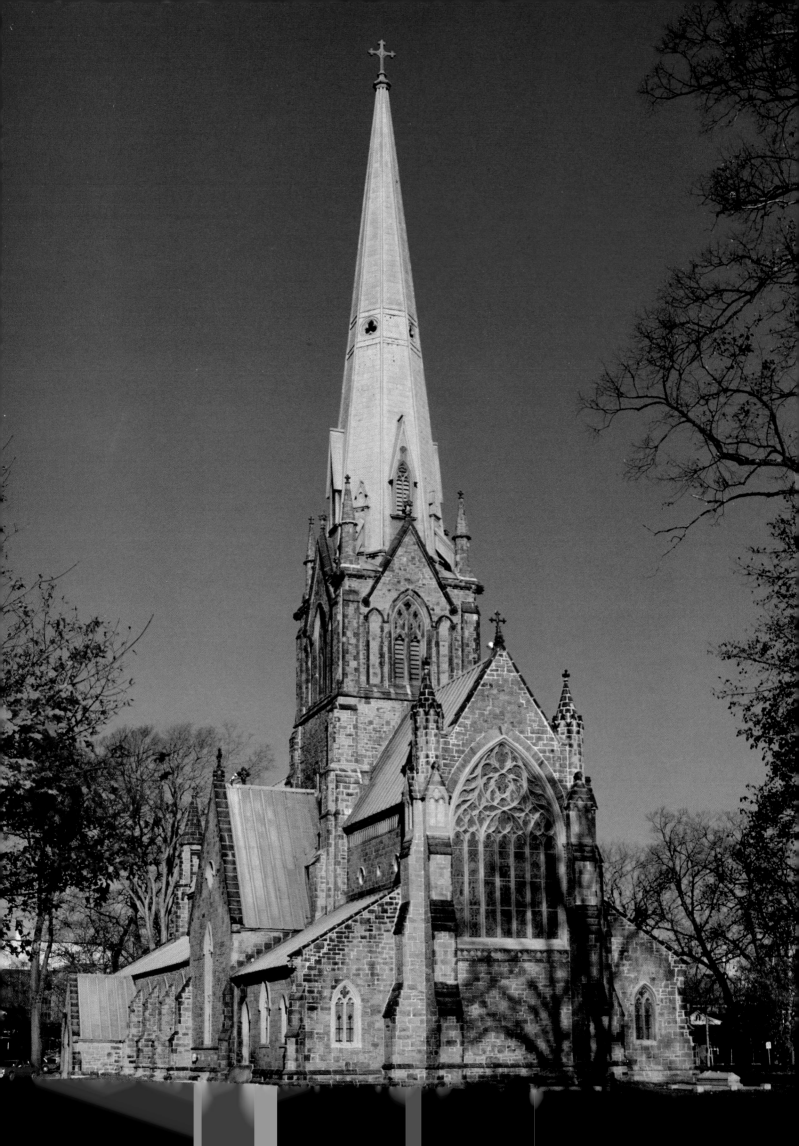

PRINCE EDWARD ISLAND

Prince Edward Island lies just beyond Northumberland Strait, only a few kilometres from New Brunswick to the west and Nova Scotia to the south. Rural? Yes, but P.E.I. is also Canada's most densely populated province. Forty percent of its landmass is under the plough: The island's unique geological characteristic — soil as red as a robin's breast — is immediately apparent. As one farmer said, "There's so much iron in the soil, it rusts!" This oxidized-iron-rich soil nurtures the healthiest potato, barley, tobacco, oat and clover plants found anywhere in the world.

Named after Prince Edward, Duke of Kent (Queen Victoria's father) in 1799, Prince Edward Island is not the title P.E.I. was given by the first European settlers. Jacques Cartier stopped here in 1534 and christened it Ile St-Jean. The Micmac Indians called this land Minegoo.

French colonists arrived on the island in 1719, supported themselves by fishing and farming, and soon became embroiled in territorial wars. In the end, British troops exiled the Acadians from Ile St-Jean. Some managed to avoid deportation and, over the years, they were joined by a few returning Acadians. Today, the west coast of Prince Edward Island is home to a small number of Acadian families, descendants of the early colonists.

Author Lucy Maud Montgomery said this was a place where "changes come more slowly . . . than. elsewhere." That may explain the peaceful farms, soft-spoken people, and the tranquility I felt when travelling through this green island. The island was once forbidden to motor vehicles, and the ban stayed in effect until 1948. It remains a place of quiet serenity with its population of about 123,000 scattered among farms and village communities.

It is possible to stay in a big name hotel and eat at a fast food restaurant here but most visitors to Prince Edward Island know that this is the kind of place where you're often better off staying in a farmhouse bed-and-breakfast and cracking claws at one of P.E.I.'s famous and frequent church-sponsored lobster suppers. At one grand community supper, my food was dished out by local ladies in a style that made me think of the good ol' days. But who cared about the good old days when right then and there the fresh lobster meat, dripping in melted butter, tasted so good!

About midway between the ferry terminal at Borden and Charlottetown is the junction with Highway 13, which goes north to Cavendish and *Anne of Green Gables* country.

Published in 1908, the novel about a red-headed orphan made Prince Edward Island famous throughout the world.

Charlottetown, with about 30,000 residents, is Canada's smallest capital city and is also one of the oldest having been capital of the province since 1763. Resting on a sheltered arm of Northumberland Strait, Charlottetown remains the kind of place you imagined Canadian cities looked like at the turn of the century. Victorian homes and buildings in the town's core have been well preserved, and the Trans-Canada runs right up to the doorstep of the most renowned of these structures — Province House. This is where, in 1864, emissaries from Upper and Lower Canada met with officials from the maritime colonies, to discuss the possibility of confederation. The self-sufficient and conservative Prince Edward Islanders chose to decline this invitation, not joining Canadian Confederation until 1873, when they could see that the kinks were starting to work themselves out. Also, the islanders were struggling with an impending bankruptcy brought on by local railway construction. Even so, Canada's Governor-General at that time, Lord Dufferin, said the islanders agreed to confederation "under the impression that it is the Dominion of Canada that has been annexed to Prince Edward Island." The room in Province House where the delegates met to confer remains, with its original furnishings, as a national monument.

The immediate surroundings include the colonial seaport of Old Charlotte Town and Great George Street. Along these well-preserved streets, cafés, shops and bookstores crowd the main floors of solid stone buildings. Entering one café, I was happy to see that I appeared to be the only tourist — everybody seemed to know everyone else in the tiny restaurant. By the time my dinner was half-cooked, the waitress (she was also the cook) had drawn me into the conversation and I knew everyone else in the place. I tried to pay for the meal with a twenty dollar bill, but she complained about having no change and insisted I accept the meal for free — on the condition that I find a good job for her if she was fired for serving free meals.

Charlottetown's famous theatre complex, Confederation Centre of the Arts, was built in 1964 to commemorate the hundredth anniversary of the meeting of the Fathers of Confederation. All provinces contributed to its construction and all help to pay for its support. Inside the complex of three theatres (one stage hosts the annual *Anne of Green Gables* musical), an art gallery, archives and a display area compensate for the building's dull grey exterior.

After Province House, the highway heads through less attractive parts of town, across a fiord of Northumberland Strait and out to the coutryside. A short drive, winding along the red-cliffed beaches of the southern island, leads to Orwell, a site rich in British heritage.

Orwell Corner is the legacy of a British surveyor who, more than two centuries ago, neatly divided the island into sixty-seven townships of roughly equal size. Each township had its "corner," providing commerce, a

Moon over grain silos near Winnipeg, Manitoba

schoolhouse and a place to meet and talk. Most of the corners have been lost to the advance of time. Orwell Corner, founded in the late 1700s by Scottish, Irish and British loyalist settlers, and named after George Orwell, England's Minister of Plantations, has survived. On Wednesdays each summer, when ceilidhs are held in the old town hall, life in the Prince Edward Island of long ago is fondly remembered and recreated. The rural crossroad looks much as it did in the late nineteenth century. Now, as then, the site has a team of Belgian draft horses who graze near the old barn.

Ruth and Ernest Taylor own a patch of land next to Orwell Corner, and are the unofficial caretakers of the hamlet. Ruth works at Orwell Corner in season as a part-time historic guide. As she explained, "We take people on the grand tour of the house, the store, post office, church, school, blacksmith's, old barn and more. It started out as a historical society by the local

people who were interested in preserving what was left of the corners. In all, I think they did a pretty good job."

Ernest looks after the Belgians, but most of his time is spent in raising and training pacers. Harness racing has ranked as the most popular sport on P.E.I. since the first official races took place over a hundred years ago. "I have a little fella here now that came out of an old hump-backed horse," he explained. "But he came out trottin'. So I started training him on a country track around here. I took him out to the track at Charlottetown after a year of training and that little two-year-old colt came in two-fifths of a second behind the winner. He coulda' won it but we didn't want to show them Charlottetown folks what he could do right off." Seeing the jet-black colt stamping and snorting around the farmyard, I had no doubt that this horse and this life were winners.

NOVA SCOTIA

In Nova Scotia, at the point where the Trans-Canada Highway crosses the Isthmus of Chignecto, the road signs declare that this is Provincial Highway 104. Here, I crossed Amherst Marsh, the glare of the setting sun filtering through the wetlands.

Just five years after Columbus landed in the Caribbean, John Cabot landed on Cape Breton Island and claimed the land for England's King Henry VII. Historians say that Leif Ericson probably landed at Yarmouth during a voyage down the North American coast in 1001, and that the Portuguese established a fishing colony at Ingonish on Cape Breton Island as early as 1521. But for the most part, until 1604, Micmac Indians were left alone with the land that was theirs in the first place. That year, the Sieur de Monts and Champlain arrived with ships of French settlers bent on permanent colonization. Samuel de Champlain, acutely aware that morale was low after hard sailing from France and even harder Canadian winters, established "L'Ordre de Bon Temps" — the Order of the Good Time. His purpose was simple: to improve the colonists' diet and spirits. Each day, a different member was appointed Grand Master and was expected to outdo previous masters in providing a grand meal and fun for the colonists. Today, the Order of the Good Time remains as North America's oldest social club.

In early years, the province — and its name — became a point of contention between the British and the French. Sir William Alexander named the peninsula Nova Scotia on being granted the territory in 1621. Of course, the French living here preferred their own name for the area — Acadia, after the explorer Verrazano's word for "peaceful land."

The English-French struggle for Nova Scotia began in 1613, when English Captain Argall landed at Port Royal to evict the French. Longfellow's epic poem of Evangeline and Gabriel relates the deportation of more than 6,500 Acadian settlers in 1755. In fact, many Acadians returned to the area after the seven years' war. One group of nine hundred *walked* from Boston through the wilderness, only to find that their homes had been taken over by colonists from Britain and New England. The wanderers finally resettled on the rugged coast of Cape Breton where, somehow, they survived. It says something about Acadian self-reliance and endurance that these people willingly lived in the most difficult parts of Nova Scotia. The Acadians chose a remote shore, put up a clapboard house, and slammed their door on the world.

Near Amherst, a turnoff heads south to Springhill, a town well known for tenacity. In 1891, a terrible blast ripped through one of Springhill's mines, splitting the shafts and taking the lives of 125 miners. In 1916 another devastating fire swept through the mines.

Thirty-nine workers were killed in an explosion and fire in 1956. Two years later an underground upheaval — a "bump" — killed seventy-six men and entombed nineteen survivors for up to eight days. Shortly afterwards Springhill's mines were closed; then two fires completely destroyed its business district. The town refused to die and Springhill today strives to be an important Nova Scotian industrial centre. Not surprisingly, Springhill has been awarded a gold medal from the Carnegie Hero Fund Commission for its courage in the face of decades of disaster.

Nova Scotian landscape is wilder than the rolling hills and tilled fields of Prince Edward Island. Here dense forests edge the Trans-Canada route and only five percent of this province's land is arable. The highway bypasses much of Nova Scotia's coast and follows the most direct route from the Isthmus of Chignecto to Cape Breton Island.

Near Truro is the exit to Pictou, landing point of the Scottish Highlanders. Over the course of ten years, a steady stream of barely-alive Highlanders stumbled off *Hector* after a gruelling eleven week journey across the Atlantic.

Three rivers that empty into Northumberland Strait at Pictou provide the area with one of Nova Scotia's strongest lobster fisheries. I began to think that lobsters were the only subject of conversation here: more than one local boasted that Nova Scotia's map outline looks something like a lobster. One person told me that even the province's weather resembles a lobster — all armour and claws.

Town names in Nova Scotia are an attraction in themselves. Antigonish and Ingonish came from the Micmac Indians who pre-dated European settlement here. At Antigonish, the campus of Saint Francis Xavier University is visible to the north of the highway. At any one time, students from eighty countries are there, majoring in co-operative and community development programs.

Near Cape Breton Island, the landscape rises into mist-shrouded mountains. (The Cape is the northern extension of the Appalachian mountain chain.) Joining mainland to Cape Breton Island, the Canso Causeway is Nova Scotia's most important engineering work of this century. Opened in 1955, the world's deepest causeway is well over a kilometre long and required more than nine million tonnes of fill for its construction.

In the heart of Cape Breton Island, on one of the Bras d'Or lakes, is Baddeck, a shipbuilding centre in the early nineteenth century, and the site of the Alexander Graham Bell National Historic Park. The park is built on a strip of land overlooking Baddeck Bay on the Bras d'Or and the Bell family properties on Beinn Bhreagh Mountain. There is a lovely light-

Log house near Perth, Ontario

house here at the edge of the bay and it was pleasant to stand in this green park with nothing but Baddeck Bay and the lighthouse in view.

The park's interpretation officer explained to me that, although the world knows Bell as the inventor of the telephone, in Baddeck he experimented with, among other projects, aviation, medical science, genetics and Canada's first hydrofoil. In 1919, Bell watched his hydrofoil speed across Bras d'Or Lake at the unprecedented rate of 114 kilometres an hour. Bell was instrumental in founding the Aerial Experiment Association, which achieved its goal when, on February 23, 1909, from the frozen surface of Bras d'Or, J.A.D. McCurdy piloted *Silver Dart*, the first powered aircraft flown in the British Empire.

Cape Breton Islanders show great affection for the inventor, not least because of the often-quoted Alexander Graham Bell comment, "I have travelled around the globe. I have seen the Canadian and American Rockies, the Andes and the Alps and the Highlands of Scotland; but for simple beauty, Cape Breton Island outrivals them all."

Where the Trans-Canada meets Baddeck, the highway follows Cabot Trail, a three-hundred kilometre road, going north to the forests and headlands of Cape Breton Highlands National Park. This circular route through northern Cape Breton Island passes through tranquil farmland and then follows the coast. Within the park are magnificent views of snug coves, craggy mountains and dense forests. The Trans-Canada Highway, on another route, climbs a different mountain. Between Baddeck and Sydney, a sign warns, "You are now at the base of Kelly's Mountain. You will climb 240 metres in the next 7 kilometres." The sign sits at sea level beside Bras d'Or Lake, and the hairpin-turned ascent of Kelly's Mountain is one of the highest and fastest climbs between here and western Alberta.

By the exit to St. Ann's, I thought of giants. In particular, Angus MacAskill, the legendary Cape Breton Giant who lived and died at St. Ann's. It wasn't difficult to get St. Ann's residents talking (and, I guessed, telling tall tales) about the giant MacAskill. A healthy 233 centimetres (7 feet, 9 inches) tall and weighing 182 kilograms (400 pounds), Angus MacAskill was known as much for his agreeable personality as for his great feats of strength — including lifting a one-ton anchor. One toothless gentleman recited his favourite MacAskill story, "An American boxer challenged young Angus to a few rounds. Angus accepted but suggested they be gentlemen and shake hands first. Before he knew it, that American had every bone in his fist crushed by the giant's grip!"

Farther up-island, I ordered lobster at a roadside restaurant near North Sydney. The sixteen-year-old waitress replied in a distinctive Cape Breton Island accent, and with a voice many years older that she, "Well, we got no lobster left! Not since the tourists be gone."

The Sydney area has been coal mining country since the French dug North America's first commercial mine in 1720, near Inverness. During much of the province's history, coal was, after fish, their greatest source of wealth. The interesting thing is that the mine shafts are under the sea. The coal seams go straight out for kilometres, and miners work beneath hundreds of metres of earth, below hundreds of metres of water. The water that leaks in is fresh, not salty. In the bowels of the earth, the men grow flowers in beds illuminated by coal mine lamps, as one miner put it, "to have some colour and life instead of just the dark."

At North Sydney, the Trans-Canada leads to a Marine Atantic ferry terminal and an eight hour journey, across the Cabot Strait to Newfoundland.

NEWFOUNDLAND

The ships of Marine Atlantic sail to Newfoundland in eight hours. While the Trans-Canada route crosses each of the western provinces in, on average, about five hundred kilometres, the route through Newfoundland is over nine hundred kilometres long — a hard day from Port aux Basques to St. John's, and another hard day's return. It was clear that the four days which I had planned to spend in Newfoundland were insufficient. And after many days on the island, it was also apparent that it can take a lifetime to truly know Canada's easternmost province.

At Port aux Basques, the Trans-Canada is known as the TCH (pronounced *de tay say haitch*). Although the Trans-Canada was opened in 1962, Newfoundland's route was not completely paved until 1965. Father of Confederation Joey Smallwood spurred his citizens on with the rallying cry "Finish the Drive in '65!" Before the Trans-Canada Highway, the only way to get an automobile from St. John's to Port aux Basques was to hoist it onto a railway car.

Even today, settlement is sparse along Newfoundland's interior route. A few small communities camp next to the highway but most Newfoundlanders still live by the sea. The Trans-Canada can't change what was determined eons ago by the Ice Age. When glaciers ground across Newfoundland, topsoil was scoured off the bedrock and deposited offshore. The debris helped to form Newfoundland's Grand Banks, the richest source of fish stocks on earth. But the island and its great hard sweeps of rock became a place to live, but not to live off the land.

Newfoundlanders think their Trans-Canada section is not as good as those in the other provinces. They're wrong. There are passing lanes and paved shoulders, just as there are on two-lane Trans-Canada routes elsewhere. It's true that when the highway officially opened in 1962, some sections of Newfoundland's route were unpaved, and it was sometimes passable only in a four-wheel drive vehicle. But today the TCH is no different in Newfoundland than in Nova Scotia, New Brunswick or Ontario. Road conditions are better here than in Northern Ontario.

At my first service station stop in Newfoundland, the attendant glanced at my car's British Columbia license plates, did something of a double take, and asked, "You come from aways, b'y? How long ye' been on the Rock?" Newfoundlanders affectionately call this bit of God's country "the Rock." Nearly as often, they call it the "precious Rock." Much of the western third of the island is made up by the northern reaches of the Appalachian mountain range and virtually all of Newfoundland is a rocky, often barren and primeval, mountainous land.

Newfoundland is an elemental place, blasted by harsh winds, bound by the high seas of the North Atlantic and remote from the North American continent. Even far-inland stretches of the Trans-Canada route can be blanketed with dense white fog. It's a hard place that nurtures tough, sociable people. These people, for the first centuries of colonization, turned their back on the barren land and built their homes overlooking the sea.

Corner Brook is the second largest city in Newfoundland and one of the few that has bucked the trend towards a sea-based economy. The community sits on a hillside, overlooking the Trans-Canada and Humber Arm of the Gulf of St. Lawrence. While mapping the west coast of Newfoundland, Captain James Cook explored Humber Arm, landed near present-day Corner Brook, and then ventured five or more kilometres up the Humber River.

Corner Brook is on a beautiful site, hugging the shoreline where the mountains roll down to the harbour and river. The community's major industrial employer, a pulp and paper mill that belches smoke into the wind over Humber Arm, rises over the highway.

Corner Brook is the access point to Blow Me Down Provincial Park. Just north of the city, the town of Steady Brook has the ski runs of Marble Mountain, the best and longest runs east of the Rockies.

The hamlet of Badger is at the half way point of Newfoundland's Trans-Canada route. Less than half an hour eastward is Grand Falls, another forestry town. Newfoundland spruce is logged extensively there and a major pulp and paper operation has, for decades, supplied newsprint to Britain. Nearby Beothuck Provincial Park is named for Newfoundland's original people. This peaceful tribe welcomed the first white settlers in the 1500s, and died regretting it. European diseases took their toll and the survivors were murdered by the colonists, many of whom hunted them for sport. The last Beothuk, a woman named Shanawdithit, died in St. John's in 1829.

The city of Gander became famous during the early year's of trans-Atlantic flight because of its low incidence of fog. Gander International Airport was built as a fuel depot, and remained the major refueling stop throughout World War II. Although modern aircraft can easily make the ocean crossing without topping up, Gander is still a stopover for aircraft experiencing unexpected headwinds, and for planes from countries where fuel costs more than in Canada.

About eighty kilometres south of Gander is Canada's most easterly National Park. Immediately inside Terra Nova National Park I read signs warning, "CAUTION, MOOSE SILHOUETTES AHEAD." Sure enough, around a sharp turn was the first of a line of life-sized, moose-shaped signs. A Park Interpreter explained that the silhouettes were first erected without a warning sign and drivers often mistook the moose silhouettes for the

Norman's Cove, St John's,
Newfoundland. **Bernard S. Jackson**

real thing, slamming on their brakes and swerving all over the highway. The park was obliged to erect signs, to warn drivers of signs that warn drivers of moose hazards. Even with the warnings, up to twenty moose are killed each year by Trans-Canada traffic. The carnage caused to animal and automobile in one of these collisions is something no one cares to see.

Located in the Upper Appalachians and the northern boreal forest, Terra Nova Park surrounds the indented shoreline and mudflats of Newman Sound, an international biological preserve where flocks of waterfowl stop during seasonal migration flights. In July, icebergs that break off from ice caps near Baffin Island, to begin a three-year journey in the Labrador Current, appear in the sound as far south as St. John's. Occasionally, an arctic fox or walrus will find itself detached from Greenland or Baffin Island and transported via iceberg to Terra Nova Park. At the same time, in Salton Bay, other migrating visitors — finback and humpback whales — can be seen.

John Cabot's explorations and landings are the subject of debate between Newfoundlanders and Cape Breton Islanders. My "interpreter," a proud descendant of a three-times-great grandfather who jumped a British Navy ship at Trinity Bay, gave Newfoundland's side of the story; "Cape Breton Islanders think that John Cabot made his first North American landfall on their island. If you talk to a Newfoundlander, however, we say that he couldn't have possibly missed Newfoundland on his way to Cape Breton Island. It's not that we say he never landed on Cape Breton . . . it's just that he must have landed on Cape Bonavista first." Newfoundlanders assert that Cabot entered this harbour on June 24, 1497 and named the bay and island after St. John (in honour of its discovery on St. John the Baptist's Day.)

As far as Europe was concerned, discovery was a story everyone wanted to hear. Cabot wrote that he found these waters "swarming with fish, which can be taken not only with the net but but in baskets let down with a stone." In Europe the news of a new food source was greeted with excitement and Cabot received a reward of ten pounds for "discovering" Newfoundland — a bonus equivalent to a ship captain's annual salary. By the time Sir Humphrey Gilbert arrived here ninety years later, Basque, Spanish and English fishing vessels crowded the harbour in Humphrey Gilbert's day — August 3, 1583 to be exact — fish stocks were so great that troops were sent to enforce Britain's claim to this "New-Founde-Lande." With the crew members from five ships and a band of musicians, Gilbert climbed to the top of Hill 'O Chips in east-end St. John's and laid the cornerstone of the British Empire. In his speech claiming British ownership, Gilbert warned that anyone committing any act prejudicial to the possession of the territory or dishonourable to Her Majesty Queen Elizabeth I would lose his ears.

The French did not listen to Gilbert's warning and, inevitably, the two countries clashed. Britain declared war on France in 1756 and during the conflict Montcalm led the French to victory in New York, the British took Louisburg, Wolfe triumphed on the Plains of Abraham and the French almost recaptured Quebec at the Battle of Sainte-Foy. Facing expulsion from the continent, the French took St. John's in June, 1762, in a last ditch attempt to retain some power. They dug themselves in on Signal Hill, with a view overlooking the narrows and harbour. Three months later, using the identical strategy Wolfe employed at Quebec City, British forces attacked overland, at Signal Hill's only unguarded flank. In a matter of minutes the French were defeated, in this last battle of the Seven Years' War. Thereafter, the island belonged to Britain. A hundred years later, Newfoundland declined an invitation to join the Dominion of Canada. After World War II, the people finally changed their minds and, on April 1, 1949, Newfoundland became part of Canada.

I found no shortage of Newfoundlanders who pointed out that the date of decision was April Fool's Day. The referendum results were an underwhelming fifty-two percent for, forty-eight percent against. That could be why the people still call themselves Newfoundlanders instead of Canadians — the oldtimers persist in calling Newfoundland a country rather than merely a province — and continue to argue over whether Canada was the right choice for them. At a church supper, one elderly gentlemen came up to me and asked if I was "the gentleman from Canada."

Signal Hill's squat stone Cabot Tower was built between 1897 and 1901 to honour Cabot and commemorate Queen Victoria's Diamond Jubilee. From the top of the tower, I saw what I had travelled almost eight thousand kilometres to see — Cape Spear, the most easterly point in North America.

South of Terra Nova, the highway touches on the arms of Trinity Bay. Picturesque fishing villages such as Clarenville, Deep Bight and Ivanys Cove come into view. This is where highway drivers become acquainted with Newfoundland's wonderful place names — the villages of Heart's Content, Little Heart's Ease, Come-By-Chance, Goobies, Tickle Bay and Dildo were my favourites.

In many of these villages, huge curving bones arch over seaside driveways. One oldtimer said that his arches are made of the jawbone of a whale. "They're easy to make," he said. "Just find yourself a whale, catch it, shoot it and take out the jawbones." At the water's edge, traditional Newfoundland fishing craft lie — forty-five-foot longliners and high-prowed dories — waiting for next year's or next day's fishing to begin. Men still go out every day from this coast and make a living catching fish.

The Trans-Canada passes through cottage country on the Avalon Peninsula, where it seems as if every St. John's family has some sort of holiday cottage set by the sea or lake shore. An old man told me that anything smaller than an ocean in Newfoundland is called a pond. Bodies of water that would be considered substantial lakes on the prairies are ponds here.

Near the eastern shore of the Avalon Peninsula, the highway turns north, bending along the contours of Conception Bay toward its final destination — St. John's — where, within the city, the Trans-Canada becomes Kenmount Road. The provincial and municipal maps all show the Trans-Canada Highway cutting north along Prince Philip Drive ending at Newfoundland's Confederation Building. But the people of Saint John's usually just say the the Trans-Canada starts "somewhere in town." Some say that "somewhere" is on Signal Hill, others say it's along Canada's oldest street, Water Street. Those people who claim the TCH starts in front of St. John's City Hall have tangible evidence to support their theory. On New Gower Street, at the entrance to St. John's city hall, is a billboard that states, "Trans-Canada Highway Mile O."

A city hall employee told me that all of the routes are more or less correct and "they all converge on the Trans-Canada Highway freeway out of town so who's to argue?" The lady then insisted that I take a grand tour of city hall, through the council chambers, past her favourite painting (of an outhouse in winter) and through the mayor's office. No one seemed concerned that a stranger was wandering into the mayor's office, barely escorted and unannounced.

The "Mile O" sign at city hall wasn't enough for me. I had to see the end of Canada at Signal Hill. The steeply-rising road to Signal Hill winds along the curving, narrow streets of Quidi Vidi Village. I imagined St. John's to be a sombre town of solid brick structures, growing out of the harbourside rock face. Instead I found Victorian wooden homes and buildings painted every bright colour imaginable. The settlement is old, and St. John's has suffered numerous fires in its history, notably in 1816, 1846 and 1892, when three-quarters of the city, including the entire business section, was wiped out. Each time the city was rebuilt, using wood. These "boxhouses" on the harbourside hills are painted bright green, dory yellow, turquoise and a host of cheerful hues.

Signal Hill was important to St. John's when lookouts stationed on the rock promontory warned of enemy ships approaching the narrow harbour. Centuries later, Guglielmo Marconi set up receivers there in a former British army barracks-turned-fever hospital, and received the first trans-Atantic radio signal.

A park interpreter at Signal Hill National Historic Park, told me that the peak is significant to Canada for more than Marconi's radio signal. "Signal Hill is a National Historic Site, as it's the site of the last battle in the Seven Years' War, in 1762," she explained. "This is where the British definitively defeated the French for possession of what was to become Canada." The visitor centre at Signal Hill investigates the history of all Newfoundland, tracing from the Viking settlements at L'Anse aux Meadows (a wind-swept plain on Newfoundland's Northern Peninsula) through five hundred years, when European colonization reached St. John's.

Trans-Canada Highway Mile "0", Saint John's Newfoundland

95

*Red Admiral butterfly nectaring near
the highway, St. John's Newfoundland*
Bernard S. Jackson

Silver Highway
Photo Contest Winner
Frozen field near Calgary, Alberta, **Stan Kruk**

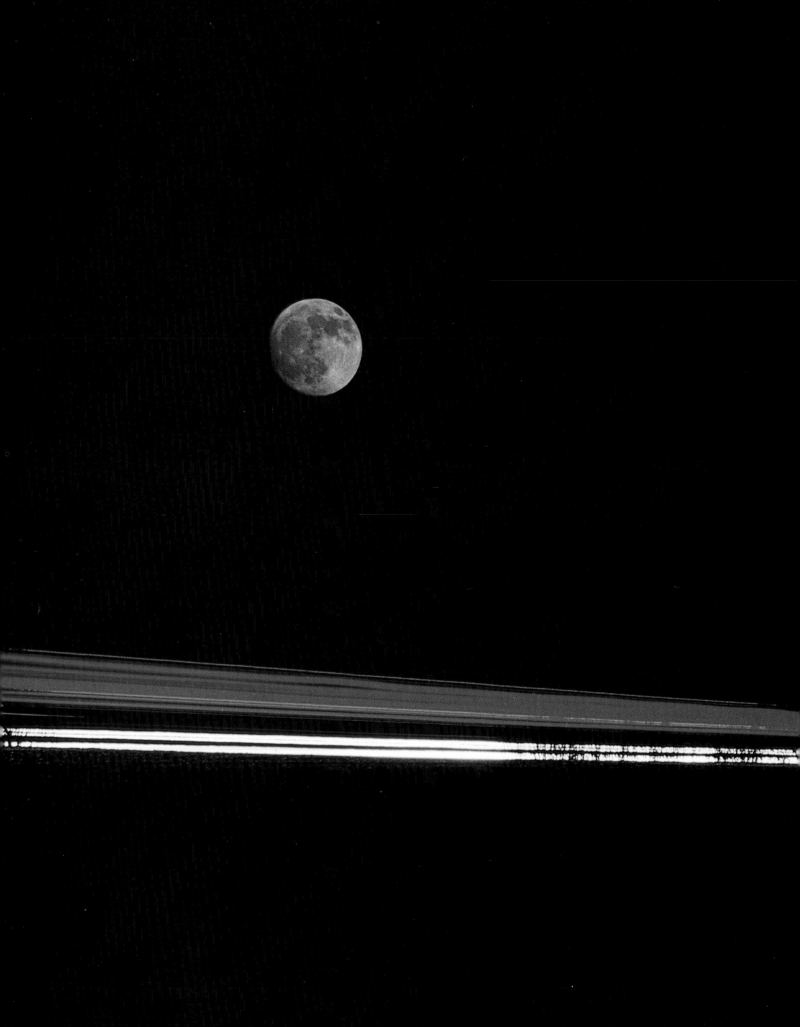

ongitudinal Centre
of Canada
96° 48' 35"

Northern Ontario, near the Trans Canada Highway. **John Devaney**

Whippletree Junction, British Columbia

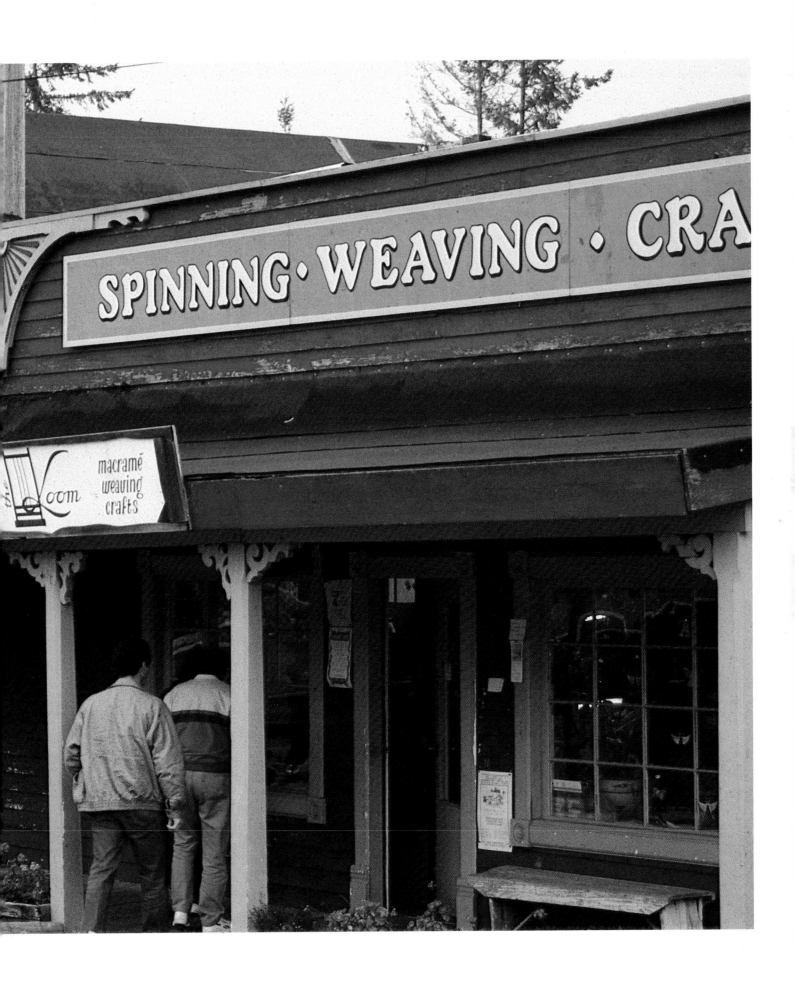

Silver Highway
Photo Contest Winner

Sulphur train, Fraser Valley by Lipton,
British Columbia, **Edna Larrabee**

Silver Highway
Photo Contest Winner

Rear view from a 16 wheeler, west side of Roger's Pass, British Columbia,
Ben Oueck

TV morning talk-show, Regina, Saskatchewan

CKCK Television sign, Regina, Saskatchewan

Silver Highway
Photo Contest Winner
*Jasper Avenue, Banff, Alberta — early
morning,* **D. Zemaitis**

Crystal Gardens, Victoria, British Columbia

Roadside derelict, Indian Head, Saskatchewan

Opposite page

Alberta's provincial animal, the pumpjack, near Brooks, Alberta

Castle Junction, Banff, Alberta

Hope, British Columbia

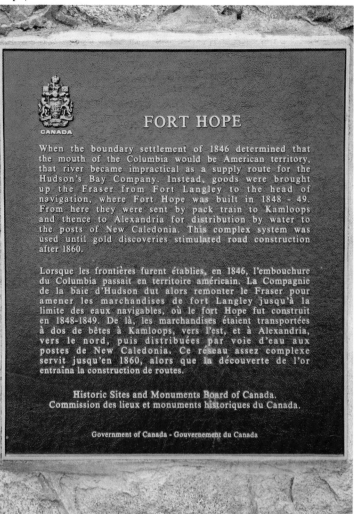

FORT HOPE

When the boundary settlement of 1846 determined that the mouth of the Columbia would be American territory, that river became impractical as a supply route for the Hudson's Bay Company. Instead, goods were brought up the Fraser from Fort Langley to the head of navigation, where Fort Hope was built in 1848 - 49. From here they were sent by pack train to Kamloops and thence to Alexandria for distribution by water to the posts of New Caledonia. This complex system was used until gold discoveries stimulated road construction after 1860.

Lorsque les frontières furent établies, en 1846, l'embouchure du Columbia passait en territoire américain. La Compagnie de la baie d'Hudson dut alors remonter le Fraser pour amener les marchandises de fort Langley jusqu'à la limite des eaux navigables, où le fort Hope fut construit en 1848-1849. De là, les marchandises étaient transportées à dos de bêtes à Kamloops, vers l'est, et à Alexandria, vers le nord, puis distribuées par voie d'eau aux postes de New Caledonia. Ce réseau assez complexe servit jusqu'en 1860, alors que la découverte de l'or entraîna la construction de routes.

Historic Sites and Monuments Board of Canada.
Commission des lieux et monuments historiques du Canada.

Government of Canada - Gouvernement du Canada

PROVINCE OF ALBERTA

MURDER OF CONSTABLE GRABURN

On November 17, 1879 new recruit Constable Marmaduke Graburn, N.W.M.P., was shot to death by an unknown assailant near the Horse Camp northwest of Fort Walsh in the Cypress Hills. Graburn was the first of the significantly few members of the force who died violently while bringing law and order to the west. The scene of his death was later named Graburn's Coulee and is now marked by a commemorative cairn in Cypress Hills Provincial Park south of here.

Constable Graburn Memorial near Medicine Hat, Alberta

Opposite page
Ashcroft Manor and Chinese coolies' home, British Columbia

W.A. Gough, violin maker, Calgary, Alberta

Madeline Saunders, owner, Ashcroft Manor, British Columbia

Silver Highway
Photo Contest Winner

*Night scene on the highway near St.
Laurent, Quebec,* **François Audy**

Previous page
Lightning storm near Lake Superior,
Ontario, **John Devaney**

Opposite page
Lower Town, Québec City

Following page
Yoho National Park, British Columbia

from above.
Hell's Gate, Fraser Canyon, British Columbia

Previous page
Terry Fox memorial, Thunder Bay,
Ontario **Bob Crosby**

Kakabeka Falls, Thunder Bay, Ontario

Silver Highway
Photo Contest Winner
Totem Pole, Victoria, B.C. **Barb McDougall**

Previous page
Silver Highway
Photo Contest Winner
Saskatchewan pool no. 6, Thunder Bay
Ontario, **Bruce Symington**

Mailbox near Mattawa, Ontario

Roadside trading post, Upsala, Ontario

Opposite page Top
Antiques etc. near Highway, British Columbia

Opposite page Bottom
Laidlaw, British Columbia "Another tourist attraction bites the dust."

Silver Highway
Photo Contest Winner

Trans-Canada Highway near Banff,
Leo MacDonald

No one else around, Stanley Park, British Columbia

Parliament Buildings, Victoria, British Columbia

Bow Falls & Banff Springs Hotel,
Banff, Alberta

Following page

Parliament Buildings, Victoria, British
Columbia

Keough's Look-out and Butter Pot
Mountains, Avalon Peninsula.
St. John's Newfoundland. **Bernard S.
Jackson**

Following page
Sunrise in Northern Ontario,
John Devaney

Hotel Bellevue, British Columbia

Following page

Fishing boats in small cove just off
Trans Canada Highway, St. John's
Newfoundland **Bernard S. Jackson**

3 9014 01567513 1